Discovery Labs in Biological Anthropology

Fatimah L.C. Jackson, Ph.D

Professor

University of Maryland
College Park, MD, USA

KENDALL/HUNT PUBLISHING COMPANY
4050 Westmark Drive   Dubuque, Iowa 52002

Contents

Foreword

The laboratories in this Manual provide an overview of human biological evolution and ecology including the biology of contemporary human groups (human biology), non-human primate social behavior (primatology), and the fossil, biochemical, and molecular evidence for human evolution (paleoanthropology). They are intended to supplement the lecture material and give you, the student, hands-on experience in the major topics of biological anthropology. The topics covered in your laboratory are organized to complement the sequence provided in lectures. In order to derive maximum benefit from these exercises, they will require your full attendance and participation in both the lectures and the laboratories. Since the laboratory has limited physical space, you need to attend the lab section in which you are enrolled.

The laboratories themselves are intended to be interesting, fun, and discovery-oriented. You should work in groups and freely discuss the labs with your classmates. However, all written work that is handed in for grading should be completed individually. Copying lab work and assignments will be considered cheating under many universities' Code of Academic Integrity.

Many people have contributed to the development of this laboratory manual since I began working on it in 1986. The initial idea of discovery labs occurred while I was teaching introductory biological anthropology at the University of Florida (1986–1990). At that time, I invented a few games such as Primate Jeopardy to help students learn some of the more difficult scientific material. When I moved to the University of Maryland in 1990, I expanded on the games and added tool-making and field reenactments on nearby National Park lands. In these activities, the creative talents of Christopher Gordon, Latifa Borgelin, and a score of other bright undergraduate and graduate teaching assistants greatly contributed to many of the laboratory exercises. Cindy Wilczak and Marilyn London also added material to this final product. Periodically I undertake revisions of this laboratory manual so that the labs reflect the most current scientific information and techniques, particularly in anthropological genetics, neurosciences, and demography. This version is the latest such revision.

Fatimah L. C. Jackson, Ph.D.
Professor and Distinguished Scholar Teacher
University of Maryland
College Park, MD (USA)
August 2006

Laboratory Safety, Bioanthropological Laboratory and Field Research Methods

Biological anthropology bridges the life sciences and the social sciences. As such, its major research methods are derived from a variety of disciplines including ecology, behavior, systematics, psychology, physiology, genetics, anatomy, sociology, evolutionary biology, etc. Understanding the methods of the discipline is crucial to appreciating its database and research perspective. This first laboratory introduces the student to biological anthropology and its laboratory and field components. We begin with an important discussion on lab and field safety. The lab then explores research techniques and the scientific methods in a laboratory exercise (extraction of DNA from a fruit) and a hypothetical field project (assessment of hamadryas baboon behavior). In both settings, biological anthropology research is grounded in the collection and analysis of quantitative and qualitative data and the interpretation of these data in an ecological and evolutionary context.

Purpose of This Laboratory

Welcome to the biological anthropology teaching laboratory. Before you begin any experiments, it is important that we review the safety rules and regulations to keep you and others safe during the various activities. These safety procedures also protect the teaching resources in the lab so that they can be used consistently. Biological anthropology is a dynamic and diverse field within anthropology. In these labs you will obtain a broad overview of the field and have the opportunity to learn many of its major concepts and methods through hands-on experiences. The labs employ work with real biological anthropology data and materials as well as simulations of field and laboratory activities.

Goals and Objectives

In this lab you will be introduced to the lab, lab policies and procedures, and to the scientific method. When you have completed this laboratory, you should be able to:

1. Understand the importance of safety in the laboratory setting and be familiar with how to respond in the event of a safety crisis.
2. Describe how to carry out and document a simple laboratory test on DNA extraction.
3. Explain how common materials can separate DNA from the cell.

Key Terms and Topics

DNA, precipitation, biological molecule, null hypothesis, alternative hypothesis, test statistic, dependent variable, independent variable, alternative hypothesis, natural selection

Pre-Lab Assignments
(do these before the beginning of this laboratory)

1. Read the information on laboratory safety and procedures and sign the safety and ethics pledge sheets.

2. Look up one or two general articles on the Internet on hamadryas baboons so you will be somewhat familiar with this species. These monkeys are the basis for our discussions and hypothetical field assessments in part 2 of this lab.

Laboratory Activities

Laboratory Activity 1: Review laboratory safety information and procedures. Tour the teaching laboratory, taking note of the locations of various safety features and exits.

The purpose of this brief overview is to promote general safety awareness, encourage safe work practices, and outline procedures for the handling and care of specimens in the lab. For more details on the safety requirements of specific laboratories, please contact your laboratory teaching assistants or your instructor. The first portion gives general guidelines that are available on the University of Maryland, Department of Environmental Safety website. The second portion deals with guidelines specific to the biological anthropology laboratory.

Basic Guidelines for Lab Safety

Awareness

The best way to prevent safety hazards is to be alert to unsafe conditions and actions, and call attention to them so that corrections can be made as soon as possible. You will notice in the teaching laboratory and prep room that all storage areas, refrigerators, and chemicals are labeled appropriately. If, during the course of an experiment, you need new chemicals, be sure to label all bottles when received and when opened. Note expiration dates on chemicals. Note special storage conditions. Be familiar with the appropriate protective measures to take when exposed to the following classes of chemicals:

- Flammables
- Radioactive compounds
- Corrosives
- Biohazards

- Toxics
- Carcinogens
- Reactives
- Compressed gases

When you are working with any of these types of chemicals, be sure to segregate the chemicals by compatibility groups for storage. Be aware of the potential interactions of lab furniture and equipment with chemicals used or stored in the lab (e.g., oxidizers stored on wooden shelving). Note any warning signs for unusual hazards such as flammable materials, biohazards, or other special problems. If you are doing experiments that require pouring chemicals, be sure to pour more concentrated solutions into less concentrated solutions to avoid violent reactions (i.e., Always add acid to water, not water to acid.).

When you are in the laboratory, avoid distracting any other worker. Practical jokes or horseplay have no place in the laboratory. Also be sure to use equipment only for its designated purpose.

Personal Safety

The most important safety concerns in the Bioanthropology Teaching Laboratory concern respiratory and general body protection. Here are a few guidelines to help maintain each:

- Fume hoods should be used whenever necessary.
- Splash proof safety goggles should be worn for eye protection (especially when making stone tools).
- Laboratory coats/aprons should be worn for general body protection (e.g., during in-class toolmaking and bioarchaeological excavations).
- Appropriate gloves should be worn as needed (e.g., latex gloves during in-class physiological experiments).
- Appropriate closed-toed shoes should be worn in the laboratory, particularly during outdoor activities and bipedalism activities.

Personal Hygiene

Here is what you can do to reduce your chances of becoming contaminated or contaminating others:

- Wash hands before leaving the laboratory.
- Wash or dry clean clothing worn in the laboratory separately from other clothing.
- Never mouth pipette anything in the laboratory. You can easily swallow whatever you are pipetting!
- Never eat, drink, or apply cosmetics in the laboratory or in areas where chemicals/hazardous agents are stored. Smoking is prohibited in all University of Maryland buildings, including this laboratory.
- Never store food in a refrigerator where hazardous materials are stored.
- Never eat or drink from laboratory glassware.
- Avoid wearing contact lenses in the laboratory.
- Avoid situating long hair, long scarfs, loose sleeves, rings, bracelets, etc., in close proximity to open flames or operating machinery.
- Keep exposed skin covered.
- Do not wear shorts, sleeveless or short sleeve shirts, or full skirts in the laboratory.

Fire Prevention

The chance of fire in the Bioanthropology Teaching Laboratory is remote; however, it is important to be aware of the potential danger. Here's what you should do as a student:

- Be aware of ignition sources in lab area (open flames, heat, electrical equipment).
- After using any flammable liquids, be sure to return them to appropriate safety cabinets and/or safety areas.
- Make sure that all electrical cords are in good condition. All electrical outlets that you are asked to use should be grounded and should accommodate a 3-pronged plug.
- Never remove the grounding prong or use an adapter to bypass the grounding on an electrical cord.

If there is a fire, you should remain out of the area of a fire or personal injury unless it is your responsibility to meet the emergency responders. Meet all responders in a safe location.
Report ALL fires by phoning 911 (telephone is located in the prep room).

Housekeeping

Whenever you are working in the laboratory, it is important that you keep the area around you clean. At the completion of every experiment, you should devote time to cleaning your work area. Here's what you can do:
- Eliminate safety hazards by maintaining laboratory work areas in a good state of order.
- Maintain at least two clear passages to laboratory exits.
- Always keep tables, fume hoods, floors, aisles, and desks clear of unnecessary material. Store books, bags, and coats underneath your work area.
- Wipe down bench tops and other laboratory surfaces after each use with an appropriate cleaning and disinfecting agent.
- Inspect all equipment before you use it.
- Keep the laboratory floor dry at all times.
- Immediately attend to spills of chemicals or water, and notify other lab workers of potential slipping hazards.

Emergency Procedures

In the event of an emergency, call 911. In the lab, you should:
→ Be familiar with the emergency evacuation plan.
→ Be aware that the names and phone numbers of lab personnel to be contacted in an emergency are posted in the lab or outside the lab door.
→ Be familiar with the location, use, and limitations of the following safety devices:

- Safety shower
- Eye wash station
- Protective respiratory gear
- Fume hood
- Spill cleanup materials
- First aid kit
- Fire alarm
- Fire extinguisher

→ Be sure to maintain a clear path to all safety equipment at all times.

Waste Disposal

Minimize wastes at the source by limiting the quantities of materials used. Dispose of all wastes in designated containers. If you have water-wet waste or heavy materials to throw away (e.g., after the tool-making laboratory), please deposit them directly into the dumpster outside Woods Hall (between Woods and Skinner Hall).

Miscellaneous Safety Information

Children and pets should *not* be brought into the laboratory. If you are doing work in the laboratory outside of your normal classroom hours, let other laboratory personnel know of your presence. If possible, avoid carrying out experimental laboratory work if Woods Hall is unoccupied.

Care and Handling of Osteological and Artifactual Specimens

The biological anthropology lab contains many valuable specimens and equipment that need to be handled with care. For both casts and real bone material you should observe the following procedures:

1. Use both hands when picking up a cranium and never lift by the zygomatic arches (cheek bones) or eye orbits (eye sockets).
2. Set skeletal material and casts on pads to prevent damage.
3. Always hold material over the lab benches; if it should slip out of your hands it is less likely to break.
4. When getting material from a box or drawer, do not "root around" for bones or casts located at the bottom. Carefully lift out the specimens on top before pulling out lower materials. This prevents damage to bones or casts when they hit or rub against one another. Gently replace material and don't try to "shove in" material that doesn't easily fit into a location.
5. When handling human skeletal material remember that these are the remains of an individual. It is a privilege to have access to these remains. Treat the material with the respect with which you would want your own skeleton to be treated.

Clean Up Your Work Area

Before you leave the lab, you should clean up your work area. This includes:

1. Picking up, wiping down, and discarding used materials and papers.
2. Sorting and replacing materials into the bags, boxes, or shelves where they were found at the beginning of the lab.
3. Pushing in your chairs and picking up materials dropped around your bench area before you leave.

Additional Rules and Regulations for Anthropology 220

1. **Standard safety procedures are to be used at all times in the laboratory.** Standard operating procedures (SOPs) are on file for all class-related laboratory activities. All laboratory personnel should be familiar with these procedures prior to beginning any work in the laboratory.
2. **The lab may only be used for class-related projects as specified in the ANTH 220 syllabus.** No external research projects are to be conducted at any time. No unauthorized persons, supplies, or equipment are permitted in the laboratory at any time. The laboratory is not a social site.
3. **Laboratory space is limited.** Only material directly related to the class activity should be brought into the laboratory. The laboratory cannot serve as a storage site for materials not connected to the assigned laboratory activity. Coats, backpacks, hats, and other items should be placed under the work tables or hung outside of the laboratory while it is in session.

4. **No eating or drinking is permitted in the laboratory except in connection with a specific class-related experiment or activity.** No food or drink is to be brought into or stored in the laboratory without the consent of the instructor.

5. **The laboratory must be kept clean at all times.** All spills and accidents must be reported immediately to the TA on duty and/or the instructor. Work area trash should not be allowed to accumulate. Each student is expected to keep his/her work area tidy.

6. **Used glassware and utensils must be washed, dried, and returned to their appropriate storage locations.** All anatomical materials must be returned to their appropriate storage locations after use. Any damaged materials must be reported immediately to the TA on duty and/or the instructor. Students will be charged for any course materials they have damaged.

7. **At the conclusion of ANTH 220, each student is expected to remove all personal items from the laboratory and to return any items borrowed from the laboratory for instructional purposes.** Students will be charged for any lost materials.

The ANTH 220 Safety Certification Sheet is located in this laboratory manual. Please sign it and turn it in to your TA at the beginning of the first lab. **There will be a safety quiz during Lab 1.**

Laboratory Activity 2: Application of the scientific method

The scientific method is a systematic approach used to study various phenomena in the natural world. The following is a summary of the steps involved in the scientific method. This example is provided from primate social behavior studies, a branch of biological anthropology.

1. **An Observation.** The scientific method starts with observation. Observations may be made from nature or from the written work of other investigators.
   FOR EXAMPLE: You observe that certain males in a number of hamadryas baboon troops appear to be subordinate to other males. The dominant males have access to and seem to consume more food weekly than do the lower ranked males. Furthermore, the dominant males appear to lose less body weight during the dry season.

2. **The Question.** From observations of the natural world, a question is developed.
   FOR EXAMPLE: Why do dominant males have greater access to and seem to consume more food than do the lower-ranked males? Why do dominant males appear to lose less body weight during times of food scarcity?

3. **The Research Hypothesis.** The question asked, observations, experience, and intuition of the researcher are used to propose a tentative explanation. This educated guess is the research hypothesis. The research hypothesis is stated in general terms.
   FOR EXAMPLE: Dominant male hamadryas baboons are able to maintain their dominance over lower-ranked males because they are better nourished especially during times of food scarcity. This may make them healthier and larger than lower-ranked males.

4. **Prediction of Results and Experimental Design.** From the general hypothesis, predictions are made about what you would expect to occur in an experimental or observational test if your general hypothesis is true vs. if it is not true. Predictions are if–then statements.
   FOR EXAMPLE: If dominant male hamadryas baboons have better access to food resources, then they should eat more. If dominant male hamadryas baboons have better access to food resources, then they lose less weight during the dry season than do lower-ranked males.

Hypotheses are then set up based on the prediction. The "straw man" " or negative case is called the null hypothesis (H_O) and the positive case is called the alternative hypothesis (H_a). In this case, we have two alternative hypotheses (H_{a-1}—which has to do with amount of food eaten and H_{a-2}—which has to do with body weight). Experiments are set up in this manner (null hypothesis versus alternative hypothesis or hypotheses) because the hypothesis testing must be in a way that allows the null hypothesis to be proven *false*. We can

→ Alternative = support
Null = negative

never prove that an alternative hypothesis is absolutely true, but we can support either or both of the alternative hypotheses if repeated experiments do not falsify them. Since we have two alternative hypotheses in this example, this is how we should set them up.

= negate

Null Hypothesis

independent = x-axis (cause)
dependent = y-axis (effect)

H_O = Dominant males eat the same amount as lower-ranked males and dominant males do not lose significantly less weight during the dry season than lower-ranked males.

°control | least amount of extraneous
#individuals

=support

Alternative Hypothesis

H_{a-1} = Dominant males eat more than lower-ranked males.
H_{a-2} = Dominant males lose significantly less weight during the dry season than lower-ranked males.

In designing an experiment to test a set of hypotheses, there are usually two variables. The first is the *independent variable* which is the factor under study. The second is the *dependent variable* which is the factor(s) being measured that responds to differences in the independent variable.

FOR EXAMPLE: Here the independent variable is male status (dominant vs. lower-ranked males) and the dependent variables are (1) amount of food consumed and (2) body weight.

In any experiment we are trying to isolate the independent variable so that it is the only factor influencing the dependent variable(s). The researcher attempts to keep all other conditions the same in the sample groups. This makes for a controlled experiment. However, it is often impossible to control all relevant variables and so there may be some variables influencing outcomes that the researcher has not even considered. This is one reason why all scientific findings are tentative and we can only support a hypothesis rather than PROVE it is true.

FOR EXAMPLE: In the hamadryas baboon experiment, one controlled variable might be age. To control for this, you would only make comparisons among hamadryas baboon males of around the same age.

5. **Perform experiments and collect data.**
   FOR EXAMPLE: Given what has been discussed so far, how might you actually test your null hypothesis? Think of specific strategies you would use to design your experiment so that you could get quantifiable measures of the dependent variables (amount of food consumed and body weight).

6. **Analyze results from the experiments.** In an experiment, the rejection or support of the null or alternative hypotheses is not always immediately apparent. Both groups under study contain individuals that vary and some of the variation within the groups of dominant and lower-status males will not be controllable. Since differences between groups are not automatically evident sometimes, we need to use another method to distinguish important differences from non-important differences.

Group results must be analyzed statistically to determine if any of the measured differences between groups are statistically significant. Statistical tests also permit us to state our results in terms of probability. This probability indicates whether the differences between groups are "authentic" (based on the independent variable) or due to chance differences. A probability statement is a measure of the magnitude of quantified differences, an assessment of the "authentic" variation within and between samples, and the sample size.

Table 1.1 provides "data" on two groups of male hamadryas baboons. Analyse these "results" and determine, using the chi-square test statistic, if the differences between the groups are statistically significant. Our level of significance will be 0.05. If you are not familiar with statistics, refer to the supplemental statistical materials presented in your Workbook. → *above 5% results happen by chance*

7. **Conclusion.** Interpret the results of the experiments to determine whether the hypotheses are supported or falsified. Since you cannot PROVE an effect, your conclusions will either be:

   a. The data reject the null hypothesis and support either one or the other or both alternative hypotheses. (Either a-1, a-2, or a-1 AND a-2)

   b. The data do not reject the null so the alternative hypotheses are NOT supported.

The results of the study of the effect of male social dominance on the amount of food eaten and the body weight during the dry season must be repeatable to be validated. This is an additional means by which researchers control for unforeseen variables, problems with equipment, measurement errors, researcher bias, etc. Sometimes, the results of an experimental or observational study may require a modification of the hypotheses and, therefore, a new experiment. Even if the conclusions appear clear-cut, they usually create several new questions for study. This is the normal means by which science progresses. Big questions are not answered in a single step; they are a series of small steps that build on previous experiments.

Control
- location
- age
- size
- environment
- food (quality and amount, availability)
- pop'n
- activity
- temperature
- all has to be done during same amount of time
  - equal # of dominant males

WRITE IN A NARATIVE WAY

*rainfall effecting the amount of food consumed
*some of the troops have less access to food
- dominance plays a part in food consumed
  *dominant males eat more than lower ranked males
  - dominant males and lower ranked males eat the same amount of food.

- How to find out dominant males eat more than the lower ranked males?

Hamadryas Baboon Hypothesis Testing Study

Table 1.1	Raw Data for Hypothesis Testing

Dominant Male Hamadryas Baboons			Lower-ranking Male Hamadryas Baboons		
Animal ID#	Amount of Food Consumed Every 2 days	Change in Body from Wet Season to Dry Season	Animal ID#	Amount of Food Consumed Every 2 days	Change in Body Weight from Wet Season to Dry Season
001	3.0 kg	−1 kg	0002	1.9 kg	−5.4 kg
003	3.3 kg	−0.9 kg	0004	2.7 kg	−3.0 kg
005	4.0 kg	−0.5 kg	0007	2.3 kg	−5.0 kg
006	2.7 kg	−1.1 kg	010	2.7 kg	−4.8 kg
124	3.4 kg	0 kg	110	4.0 kg	−4.9 kg
126	3.1 kg	−2.0 kg	121	3.9 kg	−3.5 kg
129	2.4 kg	−2.7 kg	150	4.0 kg	−2.7 kg
217	5.0 kg	−1.9 kg	218	2.8 kg	−3.8 kg
219	6.7 kg	−0.9 kg	220	3.2 kg	−7.3 kg
221	4.3 kg	−0.3 kg	236	2.2 kg	−5.9 kg
223	4.7 kg	−2.1 kg	237	3.8 kg	−3.7 kg
225	6.9 kg	−0.9 kg	249	1.9 kg	−5.0 kg
345	2.9 kg	−1.4 kg	300	3.7 kg	−6.0 kg
347	3.9 kg	0 kg	302	2.1 kg	−5.8 kg
348	3.9 kg	−2.0 kg	323	2.5 kg	−4.8 kg
349	6.4 kg	+0.1 kg	326	2.4 kg	−8.2 kg
350	3.9 kg	−0.8 kg	329	3.5 kg	−3.7 kg
355	5.5 kg	−1.5 kg	330	2.0 kg	−4.9 kg

More Information on This Data

The animal identification numbers represent specific animals observed by you over several months in the field. Four different troops of baboons are represented, as depicted below in their range map.

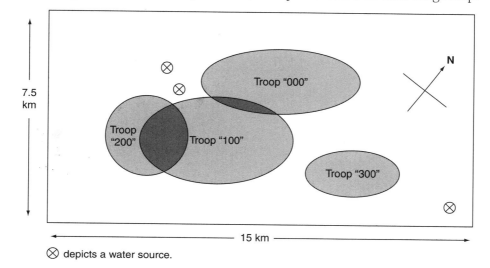

⊗ depicts a water source.

double spaced, 12 font

Post-Lab Assignment (Homework):

3 pages

(due at the beginning of the next lab)

SCENARIO: East Africa (the current countries of Kenya, Tanzania, and Uganda) is home to a large contingent of baboons. You are particularly interested in the social behavior and ecology of baboons. Imagine that you are a field bioanthropologist, working in East Africa, conducting research on the hamadryas baboons. It is hot and dusty. You've had to repair your secondhand LandRover twice. You have been tracking these animals for three months, camping whenever and wherever they settle at night and following them on foot during the day. You are now able to recognize individually adult males of four different troops. The animals tolerate your presence pretty well. All this time, you have been documenting your observations using your video camera, data from remote weighing instruments, as well as taking copious field notes. After studying these monkeys in their natural habitat, you are ready to write your first brief report on the animals. In the areas you have been making your observations there has been a protracted drought and food and water are scarce. The animals you have been studying seem to be more and more aggressive with each other as food resources dwindle. Table 1.1 represents the data you've collected to answer the specific question presented above. Type an expanded report on the results of your analysis of the data in Table 1.1 for the hamadryas baboon study. Be sure to include:

- An *introductory* paragraph that details your alternative and null hypotheses.
- A brief description of how you conducted the experiment (*methods*). ✓
- A *results* section that includes an analysis of table of raw data (Table 1.1). Calculate the mean and standard deviations for each group. Using the chi-square test statistic, determine if the differences between the *groups* are statistically significant. Use a level of significance of 0.05. If you are not familiar with statistics, refer to the statistical information provided in this laboratory manual.
- A brief *discussion* section that gives your conclusions and also describes further experiments that might be done. What uncontrolled variables might be present in this experiment?

Your report should be three pages in length, 1.5 spaced, 11 point font, single sided, 8 1/2 × 11 inches on white paper. Your report is due at the beginning of Lab 1 (next week).

2 paragraph summary w/ post-lab

uncontrolled

• genetic inheritance

observed

Chi square = 8.887

degrees of freedom = 2

P-value = 0.01175472

Expected Data

Chi - 0

df - 2

P - 1 ← can not reject null hypothesis

LAB

1

Anthropological Genetics

OBJECTIVES

- Human mitochondrial DNA (mtDNA) sequence identification
- Biological lineage coalescence
- DNA extraction from a piece of fruit
- Human DNA collection from buccal cells

Molecular genetics continues to have a profound, stimulatory effect on biological anthropology. Molecular genetic techniques are now among the most important means of hypothesis testing in biological anthropology, particularly in the fields of human biodiversity, molecular anthropology, forensic anthropology, primate conservation, and (molecular) paleoanthropology. In this laboratory, we will look for mutations in human mitochondrial DNA and we will extract DNA from a piece of fruit. In part 3 of the lab we will collect and analyze human DNA samples from buccal (cheek) cells.

Purpose of This Laboratory

The exercises in this laboratory highlight the extensive size of the human genome. The actual coding for mtDNA represents only 12% of the human genome. Within this coding you will find particular areas that are polymorphic. We've asked you to identify these areas and consider the effects of these mutations in terms of disease susceptibilities and the origin of your oldest maternal ancestor. mtDNA haplogroups have an interesting geographical distribution in the world that largely reflects the demographic movements of women. If you know where your oldest maternal ancestor came from, you probably have a good idea of which mtDNA haplogroup you may have. The concept of biological lineage is introduced to help you understand that the numbers of direct ancestors we have increase exponentially as we go back in time, but that the numbers of individuals estimated to have lived in the past decreases as we go back in time. This leads to the merging of lineages as we increasingly share ancestors, the farther we go back in time. This is known as biological lineage coalescence.

Goals and Objectives

The objective of this lab is to understand the causes and effects of human and nonhuman molecular variation through the examination of the genetic processes that influence diversity and similarity. There are four major laboratory activities:

- mtDNA assessment and discussion of mtDNA vs. nDNA
- Biological lineage coalescence
- Extraction of DNA from a piece of fruit
- Collection and analysis of human DNA from buccal cells

At the completion of this lab, you will:

- Understand more about mtDNA and be able to identify mutations in mtDNA sequences that are important in anthropological genetics.
- Understand the concept of biological lineage coalescence.
- See what DNA actually looks and feels like.
- Initiate the collection (and analysis) of your own DNA.

Key Terms and Topics

nDNA, mtDNA, gene structure, translation, transcription, base pairs, mutation, polymorphism, genotype, phenotype

Background Information on mtDNA

Humans and other animals have two types of DNA: nuclear (nDNA) and mitochondrial (mtDNA). Our nuclear DNA comes from both parents and consists of linear chromosomes. Since nuclear DNA is passed on from both parents, DNA from each parent combines to program the new organism (you!). On the other hand, your mtDNA is only from your mother and it is a circular strand of DNA found in the mitochondria of the cell. Since you get your mtDNA only from your mother, your mtDNA is exactly like that of your mother and hers is just like her mother's and so on back through time. Males cannot pass on their mtDNA to the next generation. It's maternal mtDNA all the way back so it does not undergo the kind of recombination that affects nuclear DNA.

Mitochondrial DNA is the genetic code that builds and maintains the mitochondria. Mitochondria contain enzymes that transfer energy from molecules such as glucose (derived from food) to a special energy-carrying molecule called ATP. Your cells need to carry out the chemical reactions that are necessary to maintain life and use energy carried by ATP. Mitochondria are located inside the cell in the cytoplasm but outside the nucleus. Female germ cells (ova or eggs) have cytoplasm, but male germ cells (sperm) do not. Thus you get that organ system—the mitochondria and its DNA—only from your mother.

Usually, the transmission of mtDNA and nuclear DNA from one generation to the next is 100% correct. However, once in a while—in every 100, or 1,000, or 10,000 years—a mutation occurs, probably by accident, that alters the genetic code. The longer two species have been separated, the more mutations have occurred. Therefore, if two strands of mtDNA have the same sequence with only one or two genes different, then we are looking at the same species (or family). But if we find lots of differences, then the animals are much more distantly related. Remember, the greater the differences between their DNA codes, the more time mutations have accumulated, the more distinct the organisms will be. Among humans, differences in mtDNA have been used for reconstruction of maternal ancestral origins.

The mtDNA nucleotide sequence evolves 6 to 17 times faster than comparable nuclear DNA gene sequences. This has resulted in multiple restriction fragment length polymorphisms (RFLPs), control region, and coding region nucleotide variants, as well as conformational variants and length variants. Polymorphic variants correlate with ethnic and geographic origin of the mtDNA samples, presumably because mtDNA mutations have accumulated in maternal lineages as women migrated out of Africa and into different continents. Now, there are prominent continent-specific polymorphic mtDNA variations. For example, consider mtDNA haplogroup A with np 16000–16569 modifications: 16124C, 16223T, 16319A, 16362C. This is one of many Central Asian haplotypes that is now quite common among many Native American Indian lineages.

Some mtDNA variation is associated with disease. For example, mtDNA nucleotide substitution mutants have been identified in the 16S rRNA gene, which impart resistance to the drug chloramphenicol. (This medicine is an antibiotic used to treat eye infections. Do you remember seeing this drug in your local pharmacy?) We will discuss disease relationships more in the next lab; in this lab, our focus is on ancestry and the reconstruction of maternal ancestral origins.

summary - 2 paragraphs

Laboratory Activities

Laboratory Activity 1. Human mitochondrial DNA "Cambridge" sequence

This sequence is detailed in the lines below. Find and highlight or circle seven rare polymorphisms. The polymorphisms to identify are: nucleotides 263A, 311C–315C, 750A, 1438A, 4769A, 8860A, and 15326A

mtDNA
LOCATION   **SEQUENCE OF SPECIFIC Nucleotides**

(handwritten note: polymorphism ↓ or mutation)

1	gatcacaggt ctatcaccct attaaccact cacgggagct ctccatgcat ttggtatttt
61	cgtctggggg gtatgcacgc gatagcattg cgagacgctg gagccggagc accctatgtc
121	gcagtatctg tctttgattc ctgcctcatc ctattattta tcgcacctac gttcaatatt
181	acaggcgaac atacttacta aagtgtgtta attaattaat gcttgtagga cataataata
241	acaattgaat gtctgcacag ccActttcca cacagacatc ataacaaaaa atttccacca
301	aacccccct CCCCCgcttc tggccacagc acttaaacac atctctgcca aaccccaaaa
361	acaaagaacc ctaacaccag cctaaccaga tttcaaattt tatcttttgg cggtatgcac
421	ttttaacagt cacccccaa ctaacacatt attttcccct cccactccca tactactaat
481	ctcatcaata caaccccgc ccatcctacc cagcacacac acaccgctgc taaccccata
541	ccccgaacca ccaaacccc aaagacaccc cccacagttt atgtagctta cctcctcaaa
601	gcaatacact gaaaatgttt agacgggctc acatcacccc ataaacaaat aggtttggtc
661	ctagcctttc tattagctct tagtaagatt acacatgcaa gcatccccgt tccagtgagt
721	tcaccctcta aatcaccacg atcaaaaggA acaagcatca agcacgcagc aatgcagctc
781	aaaacgctta gcctagccac accccacgg gaaacagcag tgattaacct ttagcaataa
841	acgaaagttt aactaagcta tactaacccc agggttggtc aatttcgtgc cagccaccgc
901	ggtcacacga ttaacccaag tcaatagaag ccggcgtaaa gagtgtttta gatcacccc
961	tccccaataa agctaaaact cacctgagtt gtaaaaaact ccagttgaca caaaatagac
1021	tacgaaagtg gctttaacat atctgaacac acaatagcta agacccaaac tgggattaga
1081	taccccacta tgcttagccc taaacctcaa cagttaaatc aacaaaactg ctcgccagaa
1141	cactacgagc cacagcttaa aactcaaagg acctggcggt gcttcatatc cctctagagg
1201	agcctgttct gtaatcgata aaccccgatc aacctcacca cctcttgctc agcctatata
1261	ccgccatctt cagcaaaccc tgatgaaggc tacaaagtaa gcgcaagtac ccacgtaaag
1321	acgttaggtc aaggtgtagc ccatgaggtg gcaagaaatg ggctacattt tctaccccag
1381	aaaactacga tagcccttat gaaacttaag ggtcgaaggt ggatttagca gtaaactAag
1441	agtagagtgc ttagttgaac agggccctga agcgcgtaca caccgcccgt caccctcctc
1501	aagtatactt caaaggacat ttaactaaaa cccctacgca tttatataga ggagacaagt
1561	cgtaacatgg taagtgtact ggaaagtgca cttggacgaa ccagagtgta gcttaacaca
1621	aagcacccaa cttacactta ggagatttca acttaacttg accgctctga gctaaaccta
1681	gccccaaacc cactccacct tactaccaga caaccttagc caaaccattt acccaaataa
1741	agtataggcg atagaaattg aaacctggcg caatagatat agtaccgcaa gggaaagatg
1801	aaaaattata accaagcata atatagcaag gactaacccc tataccttct gcataatgaa
1861	ttaactagaa ataactttgc aaggagagcc aaagctaaga ccccgaaac cagacgagct
1921	acctaagaac agctaaaaga gcacacccgt ctatgtagca aaatagtggg aagatttata
1981	ggtagaggcg acaaacctac cgagcctggt gatagctggt tgtccaagat agaatcttag
2041	ttcaacttta aatttgccca cagaaccctc taaatcccct tgtaaattta actgttagtc
2101	caaagaggaa cagctctttg gacactagga aaaaaccttg tagagagagt aaaaaattta

```
2161   acacccatag taggcctaaa agcagccacc aattaagaaa gcgttcaagc tcaacaccca
2221   ctacctaaaa aatcccaaac atataactga actcctcaca cccaattgga ccaatctatc
2281   accctataga agaactaatg ttagtataag taacatgaaa acattctcct ccgcataagc
2341   ctgcgtcaga ttaaaacact gaactgacaa ttaacagccc aatatctaca atcaaccaac
2401   aagtcattat taccctcact gtcaacccaa cacaggcatg ctcataagga aaggttaaaa
2461   aaagtaaaag gaactcggca aatcttaccc cgcctgttta ccaaaaacat cacctctagc
2521   atcaccagta ttagaggcac cgcctgccca gtgacacatg tttaacggcc gcggtaccct
2581   aaccgtgcaa aggtagcata atcacttgtt ccttaaatag ggacctgtat gaatggctcc
2641   acgagggttc agctgtctct tactttaac cagtgaaatt gacctgcccg tgaagaggcg
2701   ggcataacac agcaagacga gaagacccta tggagcttta atttattaat gcaaacagta
2761   cctaacaaac ccacaggtcc taaactacca aacctgcatt aaaaatttcg gttggggcga
2821   cctcggagca gaacccaacc tccgagcagt acatgctaag acttcaccag tcaaagcgaa
2881   ctactatact caattgatcc aataacttga ccaacggaac aagttaccct agggataaca
2941   gcgcaatcct attctagagt ccatatcaac aatagggttt cgacctcga tgttggatca
3001   ggacatcccg atggtgcagc cgctattaaa ggttcgtttg ttcaacgatt aaagtcctac
3061   gtgatctgag ttcagaccgg agtaatccag gtcggtttct atcta-cttc aaattcctcc
3121   ctgtacgaaa ggacaagaga aataaggcct acttcacaaa gcgccttccc ccgtaaatga
3181   tatcatctca acttagtatt atacccacac ccacccaaga acagggtttg ttaagatggc
3241   agagcccggt aatcgcataa aacttaaaac tttacagtca gaggttcaat tcctcttctt
3301   aacaacatac ccatggccaa cctcctactc ctcattgtac ccattctaat cgcaatggca
3361   ttcctaatgc ttaccgaacg aaaaattcta ggctatatac aactacgcaa aggccccaac
3421   gtTgtaggcc cctacgggct actacaaccc ttcgctgacg ccataaaact cttcaccaaa
3481   gagcccctaa aacccgccac atctaccatc accctctaca tcaccgcccc gaccttagct
3541   ctcaccatcg ctcttctact atgaaccccc ctccccatac ccaacccct ggtcaacctc
3601   aacctaggcc tcctatttat tctagccacc tctagcctag ccgtttactc aatcctctga
3661   tcagggtgag catcaaactc aaactacgcc ctgatcggcg cactgcgagc agtagcccaa
3721   acaatctcat atgaagtcac cctagccatc attctactat caacattact aataagtggc
3781   tcctttaacc tctccaccct tatcacaaca caagaacacc tctgattact cctgccatca
3841   tgaccccttgg ccataatatg atttatctcc acactagcag agaccaaccg aacccccttc
3901   gaccttgccg aaggggagtc cgaactagtc tcaggcttca acatcgaata cgccgcaggc
3961   cccttcgccc tattcttcat agccgaatac acaaacatta ttataataaa caccctcacc
4021   actacaatct tcctaggaac aacatatgac gcactctccc ctgaactcta cacaacatat
4081   tttgtcacca agaccctact tctaacctcc ctgttcttat gaattcgaac agcatacccc
4141   cgattccgct acgaccaact catacacctc ctatgaaaaa acttcctacc actcacccta
4201   gcattactta tatgatatgt ctccataccc attacaatct ccagcattcc ccctcaaacc
4261   taagaaatat gtctgataaa agagttactt tgatagagta aataatagga gcttaaaccc
4321   ccttatttct aggactatga gaatcgaacc catccctgag aatccaaaat tctccgtgcc
4381   acctatcaca ccccatccta aagtaaggtc agctaaataa gctatcgggc ccataccccg
4441   aaaatgttgg ttatacccct cccgtactaa ttaatcccct ggcccaaccc gtcatctact
4501   ctaccatctt tgcaggcaca ctcatcacag cgctaagctc gcactgattt tttacctgag
4561   taggcctaga aataaacatg ctagctttta ttccagttct aaccaaaaaa ataaaccctc
4621   gttccacaga agctgccatc aagtatttcc tcacgcaagc aaccgcatcc ataatccttc
4681   taatagctat cctcttcaac aatatactct ccggacaatg aaccataacc aatactacca
4741   atcaatactc atcattaata atcataatAg ctatagcaat aaaactagga atagcccccct
4801   ttcacttctg agtcccagag gttacccaag gcacccctct gacatccggc ctgcttcttc
4861   tcacatgaca aaaactagcc cccatctcaa tcatatacca aatctctccc tcactaaacg
4921   taagccttct cctcactctc tcaatcttat ccatcatagc aggcagttga ggtggattaa
4981   accaAaccca gctacgcaaa atcttagcat actcctcaat tacccacata ggatgaataa
5041   tagcagttct accgtacaac cctaacataa ccattcttaa tttaactatt tatattatcc
```

```
5101    taactactac cgcattccta ctactcaact taaactccag caccacgacc ctactactat
5161    ctcgcacctg aaacaagcta acatgactaa caccctaat tccatccacc ctcctctccc
5221    taggaggcct gcccccgcta accggctttt tgcccaaatg ggccattatc gaagaattca
5281    caaaaaacaa tagcctcatc atccccacca tcatagccac catcaccctc cttaacctct
5341    acttctacct acgcctaatc tactccacct caatcacact actccccata tctaacaacg
5401    taaaaataaa atgacagttt gaacatacaa aacccacccc attcctcccc acactcatcg
5461    cccttaccac gctactccta cctatctccc cttttatact aataatctta tagaaattta
5521    ggttaaatac agaccaagag ccttcaaagc cctcagtaag ttgcaatact taatttctgt
5581    aacagctaag gactgcaaaa ccccactctg catcaactga acgcaaatca gccactttaa
5641    ttaagctaag cccttactag accaatggga cttaaaccca caaacactta gttaacagct
5701    aagcacccta atcaactggc ttcaatctac ttctcccgcc gccgggaaaa aaggcgggag
5761    aagcccggc aggtttgaag ctgcttcttc gaatttgcaa ttcaatatga aaatcacctc
5821    ggagctggta aaaagaggcc taacccctgt ctttagattt acagtccaat gcttcactca
5881    gccattttac ctcacccca ctgatgttcg ccgaccgttg actattctct acaaaccaca
5941    aagacattgg aacactatac ctattattcg gcgcatgagc tggagtccta ggcacagctc
6001    taagcctcct tattcgagcc gagctgggcc agccaggcaa ccttctaggt aacgaccaca
6061    tctacaacgt tatcgtcaca gcccatgcat ttgtaataat cttcttcata gtaatacca
6121    tcataatcgg aggctttggc aactgactag ttccctaat aatcggtgcc cccgatatgg
6181    cgtttcccg cataaacaac ataagcttct gactcttacc tccctctctc ctactcctgc
6241    tcgcatctgc tatagtggag gccggagcag gaacaggttg aacagtctac cctcccttag
6301    cagggaacta ctcccaccct ggagcctccg tagacctaac catcttctcc ttacacctag
6361    caggtgtctc ctctatctta ggggccatca atttcatcac aacaattatc aatataaaac
6421    ccctgccat aacccaatac caaacgcccc tcttcgtctg atccgtccta atcacagcag
6481    tcctacttct cctatctctc ccagtcctag ctgctggcat cactatacta ctaacagacc
6541    gcaacctcaa caccaccttc ttcgacccg ccggaggagg agaccccatt ctataccaac
6601    acctattctg attttttcggt caccctgaag tttatattct tatcctacca ggcttcggaa
6661    taatctccca tattgtaact tactactccg gaaaaaaaga accatttgga tacataggta
6721    tggtctgagc tatgatatca attggcttcc tagggtttat cgtgtgagca caccatatat
6781    ttacagtagg aatagacgta gacacacgag catatttcac ctccgctacc ataatcatcg
6841    ctatccccac cggcgtcaaa gtatttagct gactcgccac actccacgga agcaatatga
6901    aatgatctgc tgcagtgctc tgagccctag gattcatctt tcttttcacc gtaggtggcc
6961    tgactggcat tgtattagca aactcatcac tagacatcgt actacacgac acgtactacg
7021    ttgtagccca cttccactat gtcctatcaa taggagctgt atttgccatc ataggaggct
7081    tcattcactg atttccccta ttctcaggct acaccctaga ccaaacctac gccaaaatcc
7141    atttcactat catattcatc ggcgtaaatc taactttctt cccacaacac tttctcggcc
7201    tatccggaat gccccgacgt tactcggact accccgatgc atacaccaca tgaaacatcc
7261    tatcatctgt aggctcattc atttctctaa cagcagtaat attaataatt ttcatgattt
7321    gagaagcctt cgcttcgaag cgaaaagtcc taatagtaga agaaccctcc ataaacctgg
7381    agtgactata tggatgcccc ccaccctacc acacattcga agaacccgta tacataaaat
7441    ctagacaaaa aaggaaggaa tcgaacccc caaagctggt ttcaagccaa ccccatggcc
7501    tccatgactt tttcaaaaag gtattagaaa aaccatttca taactttgtc aaagttaaat
7561    tataggctaa atcctatata tcttaatggc acatgcagcg caagtaggtc tacaagacgc
7621    tacttcccct atcatagaag agcttatcac ctttcatgat cacgccctca taatcatttt
7681    ccttatctgc ttcctagtcc tgtatgccct tttcctaaca ctcacaacaa aactaactaa
7741    tactaacatc tcagacgctc aggaaataga aaccgtctga actatcctgc ccgccatcat
7801    cctagtcctc atcgccctcc catccctacg catcctttac ataacagacg aggtcaacga
7861    tccctccctt accatcaaat caattggcca ccaatggtac tgaacctacg agtacaccga
7921    ctacggcgga ctaatcttca actcctacat acttcccca ttattcctag aaccaggcga
7981    cctgcgactc cttgacgttg acaatcgagt agtactcccg attgaagccc ccattcgtat
```

```
8041   aataattaca tcacaagacg tcttgcactc atgagctgtc cccacattag gcttaaaaac
8101   agatgcaatt cccggacgtc taaaccaaac cactttcacc gctacacgac cggggggtata
8161   ctacggtcaa tgctctgaaa tctgtggagc aaaccacagt ttcatgccca tcgtcctaga
8221   attaattccc ctaaaaatct ttgaaatagg gcccgtattt accctatagc acccctctta
8281   ccccctctag agcccactgt aaagctaact tagcattaac cttttaagtt aaagattaag
8341   agaaccaaca cctctttaca gtgaaatgcc ccaactaaat actaccgtat ggcccaccat
8401   aattacccc atactcctta cactattcct catcacccaa ctaaaaatat taaacacaaa
8461   ctaccaccta cctccctcac caaagcccat aaaaataaaa aattataaca aaccctgaga
8521   accaaaatga acgaaaatct gttcgcttca ttcattgccc ccacaatcct aggcctaccc
8581   gccgcagtac tgatcattct atttccccct ctattgatcc ccacctccaa atatctcatc
8641   aacaaccgac taatcaccac ccaacaatga ctaatcaaac taacctcaaa acaaatgata
8701   accatacaca acactaaagg acgaacctga tctcttatac tagtatcctt aatcattttt
8761   attgccacaa ctaacctcct cggactcctg cctcactcat ttacaccaac cacccaacta
8821   tctataaacc tagccatggc catccccta tgagcgggcA cagtgattat aggctttcgc
8881   tctaagatta aaaatgccct agcccacttc ttaccacaag gcacacctac accccttatc
8941   cccatactag ttattatcga aaccatcagc ctactcattc aaccaatagc cctggccgta
9001   cgcctaaccg ctaacattac tgcaggccac ctactcatgc acctaattgg aagcgccacc
9061   ctagcaatat caaccattaa ccttccctct acacttatca tcttcacaat tctaattcta
9121   ctgactatcc tagaaatcgc tgtcgcctta atccaagcct acgtttttcac acttctagta
9181   agcctctacc tgcacgacaa cacataatga cccaccaatc acatgcctat catatagtaa
9241   aacccagccc atgaccccta acaggggccc tctcagccct cctaatgacc tccggcctag
9301   ccatgtgatt tcacttccac tccataacgc tcctcatact aggcctacta accaacacac
9361   taaccatata ccaatgatgg cgcgatgtaa cacgagaaag cacataccaa ggccaccaca
9421   caccacctgt ccaaaaaggc cttcgatacg ggataatcct atttattacc tcagaagttt
9481   ttttcttcgc aggatttttc tgagcctttt accactccag cctagcccct acccccaat
9541   taggagggca ctggcccCa acaggcatca ccccgctaaa tccccctagaa gtcccactcc
9601   taaacacatc cgtattactc gcatcaggag tatcaatcac ctgagctcac catagtctaa
9661   tagaaaacaa ccgaaaccaa ataattcaag cactgcttat tacaattta ctgggtctct
9721   attttacccct cctacaagcc tcagagtact tcgagtctcc cttcaccatt tccgacggca
9781   tctacggctc aacatttttt gtagccacag gcttccacgg acttcacgtc attattggct
9841   caactttcct cactatctgc ttcatccgcc aactaatatt tcactttaca tccaaacatc
9901   actttggctt cgaagccgcc gcctgatact ggcattttgt agatgtggtt tgactatttc
9961   tgtatgtctc catcattga tgagggtctt actctttag tataaatagt accgttaact
10021  tccaattaac tagttttgac aacattcaaa aaagagtaat aaacttcgcc ttaattttaa
10081  taatcaacac cctcctagcc ttactactaa taattattac attttgacta ccacaactca
10141  acggctacat agaaaaatcc acccccttacg agtgcggctt cgaccctata tccccgccc
10201  gcgtcccttt ctccataaaa ttcttcttag tagctattac cttcttatta tttgatctag
10261  aaattgccct cctttaccc ctaccatgag ccctacaaac aactaacctg ccactaatag
10321  ttatgtcatc cctcttatta atcatcatcc tagccctaag tctggcctat gagtgactac
10381  aaaaaggatt agactgaacc gaattggtat atagtttaaa caaaacgaat gatttcgact
10441  cattaaatta tgataatcat atttaccaaa tgcccctcat ttacataaat attatactag
10501  catttaccat ctcacttcta ggaatactag tatatcgctc acacctcata tcctccctac
10561  tatgcctaga aggaataata ctatcgctgt tcattatagc tactctcata accctcaaca
10621  cccactccct cttagccaat attgtgccta ttgccatact agtctttgcc gcctgcgaag
10681  cagcggtggg cctagcccta ctagtctcaa tctccaacac atatggccta gactacgtac
10741  ataacctaaa cctactccaa tgctaaaact aatcgtccca acaattatat tactaccact
10801  gacatgactt tccaaaaaac acataatttg aatcaacaca accacccaca gcctaattat
10861  tagcatcatc cctctactat tttttaacca aatcaacaac aacctattta gctgttcccc
10921  aacctttcc tccgaccccc taacaacccc cctcctaata ctaactacct gactcctacc
```

```
10981   cctcacaatc atggcaagcc aacgccactt atccagtgaa ccactatcac gaaaaaaact
11041   ctacctctct atactaatct ccctacaaat ctccttaatt ataacattca cagccacaga
11101   actaatcata ttttatatct tcttcgaaac cacacttatc cccaccttgg ctatcatcac
11161   ccgatgaggc aaccagccag aacgcctgaa cgcaggcaca tacttcctat tctacaccct
11221   agtaggctcc cttcccctac tcatcgcact aatttacact cacaacaccc taggctcact
11281   aaacattcta ctactcactc tcactgccca agaactatca aactcctgag ccaaCaactt
11341   aatatgacta gcttacacaa tagctttat agtaaagata cctctttacg gactccactt
11401   atgactccct aaagcccatg tcgaagcccc catcgctggg tcaatagtac ttgccgcagt
11461   actcttaaaa ctaggcggct atggtataat acgcctcaca ctcattctca acccctgac
11521   aaaacacata gcctacccct tccttgtact atccctatga ggcataatta taacaagctc
11581   catctgccta cgacaaacag acctaaaatc gctcattgca tactcttcaa tcagccacat
11641   agccctcgta gtaacagcca ttctcatcca aaccccctga agcttcaccg gcgcagtcat
11701   tctcataatc gcccacgggc ttacatcctc attactattc tgcctagcaa actcaaacta
11761   cgaacgcact cacagtcgca tcataatcct ctctcaagga cttcaaactc tactcccact
11821   aatagctttt tgatgacttc tagcaagcct cgctaacctc gccttacccc ccactattaa
11881   cctactggga gaactctctg tgctagtaac cacgttctcc tgatcaaata tcactctcct
11941   acttacagga ctcaacatac tagtcacagc cctatactcc ctctacatat ttaccacaac
12001   acaatggggc tcactcaccc accacattaa caacataaaa ccctcattca cacgagaaaa
12061   caccctcatg ttcatacacc tatcccccat tctcctccta tccctcaacc ccgacatcat
12121   taccgggttt tcctcttgta aatatagttt aaccaaaaca tcagattgtg aatctgacaa
12181   cagaggctta cgacccctta tttaccgaga aagctcacaa gaactgctaa ctcatgcccc
12241   catgtctaac aacatggctt tctcaacttt taaaggataa cagctatcca ttggtcttag
12301   gccccaaaaa ttttggtgca actccaaata aaagtaataa ccatgcacac tactataacc
12361   accctaaccc tgacttccct aattcccccc atccttacca ccctcgttaa ccctaacaaa
12421   aaaaactcat acccccatta tgtaaaatcc attgtcgcat ccacctttat tatcagtctc
12481   ttccccacaa caatattcat gtgcctagac caagaagtta ttatctcgaa ctgacactga
12541   gccacaaccc aaacaaccca gctctcccta agcttcaaac tagactactt ctccataata
12601   ttcatccctg tagcattgtt cgttacatgg tccatcatag aattctcact gtgatatata
12661   aactcagacc caaacattaa tcagttcttc aaatatctac tcatcttcct aattaccata
12721   ctaatcttag ttaccgctaa caacctattc caactgttca tcggctgaga gggcgtagga
12781   attatatcct tcttgctcat cagttgatga tacgcccgag cagatgccaa cacagcagcc
12841   attcaagcaa tcctatacaa ccgtatcggc gatatcggtt tcatcctcgc cttagcatga
12901   tttatcctac actccaactc atgagaccca caacaaatag cccttctaaa cgctaatcca
12961   agcctcaccc cactactagg cctcctccta gcagcagcag gcaaatcagc ccaattaggt
13021   ctccacccct gactcccctc agccatagaa ggccccaccc cagtctcagc cctactccac
13081   tcaagcacta tagttgtagc aggaatcttc ttactcatcc gcttccaccc cctagcagaa
13141   aatagcccac taatccaaac tctaacacta tgcttaggcg ctatcaccac tctgttcgca
13201   gcagtctgcg cccttacaca aaatgacatc aaaaaaatcg tagccttctc cacttcaagt
13261   caactaggac tcataatagt tacaatcggc atcaaccaac cacacctagc attcctgcac
13321   atctgtaccc acgccttctt caaagccata ctatttatgt gctccgggtc catcatccac
13381   aaccttaaca atgaacaaga tattcgaaaa ataggaggac tactcaaaac catacctctc
13441   acttcaacct ccctcaccat tggcagccta gcattagcag gaataccttt cctcacaggt
13501   ttctactcca aagaccacat catcgaaacc gcaaacatat catacacaaa cgcctgagcc
13561   ctatctatta ctctcatcgc tacctccctg acaagcgcct atagcactcg aataattctt
13621   ctcaccctaa caggtcaacc tcgcttcccc acccttacta acattaacga aaataacccc
13681   accctactaa accccattaa aCgcctggca gccggaagcc tattcgcagg atttctcatt
13741   actaacaaca tttcccccgc atcccccttc caaacaacaa tccccctcta cctaaaactc
13801   acagccctcg ctgtcacttt cctaggactt ctaacagccc tagacctcaa ctacctaacc
13861   aacaaactta aaataaaatc cccactatgc acattttatt tctccaacat actcggattc
```

```
13921   taccctagca tcacacaccg cacaatcccc tatctaggcc ttcttacgag ccaaaacctg
13981   cccctactcc tcctagacct aacctgacta gaaaagctat tacctaaaac aatttcacag
14041   caccaaatct ccacctccat catcacctca acccaaaaag gcataattaa actttacttc
14101   ctctctttct tcttcccact catcctaacc ctactcctaa tcacataacc tattcccccg
14161   agcaatctca attacaatat atacaccaac aaacaatgTt caaccagtaa ctactactaa
14221   tcaacgccca taatcataca aagcccccgc accaatagga tcctcccgaa tCaaccctga
14281   cccctctcct tcataaatta ttcagcttcc tacactatta aagtttacca caaccaccac
14341   cccatcatac tctttcaccc acagCacCaa tcctacctcc atcgctaacc ccactaaaac
14401   actcaccaag acctcaaccc ctgacccca tgcctcagga tactcctcaa tagccatcgc
14461   tgtagtatat ccaaagacaa ccatcattcc ccctaaataa attaaaaaaa ctattaaacc
14521   catataacct cccccaaaat tcagaataat aacacacccg accacaccgc taacaatcaa
14581   tactaaaccc ccataaatag gagaaggctt agaagaaaac cccacaaacc ccattactaa
14641   acccacactc aacagaaaca aagcatacat cattattctc gcacggacta caaccacgac
14701   caatgatatg aaaaaccatc gttgtatttc aactacaaga acaccaatga ccccaatacg
14761   caaaaCtaac cccctaataa aattaattaa ccactcattc atcgacctcc ccaccccatc
14821   caacatctcc gcatgatgaa acttcggctc actccttggc gcctgcctga tcctccaaat
14881   caccacagga ctattcctag ccatgcacta ctcaccagac gcctcaaccg ccttttcatc
14941   aatcgcccac atcactcgag acgtaaatta tggctgaatc atccgctacc ttcacgccaa
15001   tggcgcctca atattcttta tctgcctctt cctacacatc gggcgaggcc tatattacgg
15061   atcatttctc tactcagaaa cctgaaacat cggcattatc ctcctgcttg caactatagc
15121   aacagccttc ataggctatg tcctcccgtg aggccaaata tcattctgag gggccacagt
15181   aattacaaac ttactatccg ccatcccata cattgggaca gacctagttc aatgaatctg
15241   aggaggctac tcagtagaca gtcccacccct cacacgattc tttacctttc acttcatctt
15301   gcccttcatt attgcagccc tagcaAcact ccacctccta ttcttgcacg aaacgggatc
15361   aaacaacccc ctaggaatca cctcccattc cgataaaatc accttccacc cttactacac
15421   aatcaaagac gccctcggct tacttctctt ccttctctcc ttaatgacat taacactatt
15481   ctcaccagac ctcctaggcg acccagacaa ttatacccta gccaaccct taaacacccc
15541   tccccacatc aagcccgaat gatatttcct attcgcctac acaattctcc gatccgtccc
15601   taacaaacta ggaggcgtcc ttgccctatt actatccatc ctcatcctag caataatccc
15661   catcctccat atatccaaac aacaaagcat aatatttcgc ccactaagcc aatcactta
15721   ttgactccta gccgcagacc tcctcattct aacctgaatc ggaggacaac cagtaagcta
15781   ccctttacc atcattggac aagtagcatc cgtactatac ttcacaacaa tcctaatcct
15841   aataccaact atctccctaa ttgaaaacaa aatactcaaa tgggcctgtc cttgtagtat
15901   aaactaatac accagtcttg taaaccggag atgaaaacct ttttccaagg acaaatcaga
15961   gaaaaagtct ttaactccac cattagcacc caaagctaag attctaattt aaactattct
16021   ctgttctttc atggggaagc agatttgggt accacccaag tattgactca cccatcaaca
16081   accgctatgt atttcgtaca ttactgccag ccaccatgaa tattgtacgg taccataaat
16141   acttgaccac ctgtagtaca taaaaaccca atccacatca aaaccccctc cccatgctta
16201   caagcaagta cagcaatcaa ccctcaacta tcacacatca actgcaactc caaagccacc
16261   cctcacccac taggatacca acaaacctac ccacccttaa cagtacatag tacataaagc
16321   catttaccgt acatagcaca ttacagtcaa atcccttctc gtccccatgg atgacccccc
16381   tcagataggg gtcccttgac caccatcctc cgtgaaatca atatcccgca caagagtgct
16441   actctcctcg ctccgggccc ataacacttg ggggtagcta aagtgaactg tatccgacat
16501   ctggttccta cttcagggtc ataaagccta aatagcccac acgttcccct taaataagac
16561   atcacgatg

BASE COUNT (16569 total):   5124 a        5181 c        2169 g        4094 t
```

Laboratory Activity 2. The concept of biological lineage coalescence

Examine the diagram presented below and discuss why the number of direct biological ancestors increases as you go back in time while the number of potential ancestors actually decreases as you go back in time.

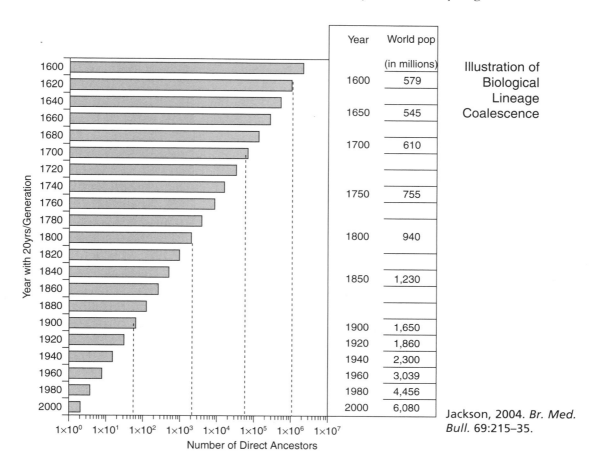

Jackson, 2004. *Br. Med. Bull.* 69:215–35.

Laboratory Activity 3. Application of the scientific method to anthropological genetics

In this part of the lab, each student will follow a basic scientific protocol to extract DNA from a piece of fruit. Be sure to keep good notes on all of your observations and answer the questions presented throughout the exercise. The answers to these questions will be discussed during this laboratory.

Experiment: Extracting DNA from Fruit

Introduction

DNA is present in the cells of all living organisms. This exercise is designed to extract DNA from fruit in sufficient quantity to be seen and spooled. Each student will have a tube of DNA at the end that they can take home with them.

In-Lab Activity: Answer each of the following questions and be prepared to discuss your answers during the lab.

One way to purify a molecule is to get rid of everything but that molecule.

QUESTION 1: If we want to isolate DNA from fruit, what do we have to get rid of?
-separate the DNA from the fruit

QUESTION 2: What materials would you use to do that?

QUESTION 3: What can we do with the DNA once we've purified it?
- study it
- put under microscope

Materials

- Ziplock bags (1 per student)
- Extraction solution (1 test tube of about 8 ml per student) (This is our cell lysis solution!)
- Funnel that fits test tube (1 per student pair)
- Cheesecloth (1 per student, cut to cover the funnel)
- Fruit (1 per student)
- Cold 95% ethanol or isopropanol (about 5 ml per student) (This is our precipitation solution!)
- Extra test tube (should be able to hold about 15 ml)
- Glass rod

Extraction Solution Recipe

For one liter of the extraction solution, mix 100 ml of shampoo and 15 g of table salt. Add water to make a final volume of 1 liter. Dissolve the salt by stirring slowly to avoid foaming. Measure 8 ml of solution for each student. Your instructional staff has already prepared this solution for you and placed 8 ml in a conical test tube. Use this solution as your cell lysis solution.

Protocol

1. **Get a piece of fruit and put it in a ziplock bag.** Recommended fruits include strawberries or bananas. Mash the fruit thoroughly but carefully, about 5 minutes, so that the bag does not break.

QUESTION 4: What does crushing the fruit do? breaking the cell membrane

2. **Add 8 ml of extraction solution to the ziplock bag.** Make sure the bag is closed without much extra air.

salt will precipitate the DNA

QUESTION 5: What do you think the extraction solution does to the mashed fruit? - breaks it up
*Salt is positively charged and DNA is negatively charged so the salt helps to draw out the DNA

3. **Place a funnel on top of a test tube and cover with cheesecloth. Filter the mixture through the cheesecloth.**

QUESTION 6: What is being filtered out?
the solids and pulp are being filtered from the liquid

QUESTION 7: What is going through the filter?

-All the cell parts are being caught by the filter and the liquids are going through the filter

4. Pour about half of the "fruit juice" plus extraction solution into a second test tube so that each student has his or her own test tube with 8–9 ml of cell lysis solution in each.

5. Being careful not to shake the tubes, add approximately 5 ml of cold 95% ethanol to each tube.

QUESTION 8: What do you think the ethanol does?

- DNA not soluble in alcohol; separates the DNA

QUESTION 9: Why do we want it cold?

- the cold alcohol helps to protect the DNA and will help to precipitate the DNA from the rest of the solution.

6. Take a look at your tube.

QUESTION 10: What do you see in the top portion of the liquid?

- we see the DNA floating at the top of the tube

7. Write down all of your observations and answer each QUESTION to the best of your ability. We will go over the answers in lab.

Laboratory Activity 4. Human DNA collection from one buccal brush

Complete the ancestry survey and place this in the brown coin envelope. Make sure that the number on the survey and the number on the coin envelope are identical.

Remove any food or other foreign organic materials from your mouth. If you have recently consumed coffee, please rinse your mouth with clean water before continuing with this part of the lab.

Carefully remove the sterile nylon bristle cytological brush from its container. Do not discard the container. Immediately place the brush in your mouth. (Don't touch the brush with your hands or place the brush on any surface!) Scrape the inside of your cheek 10 times with the brush and return the buccal brush to the original container, placing the brush end first.

Make sure that your individual number is located on the container holding the inoculated buccal brush. Place the buccal brush container with the brush inside into the coin envelope. Make sure that the number on the coin envelope and the number on the brush container are identical. Keep a copy of your individual number in a secure location. No names will be associated with individual samples; only you will know which sample is yours. Turn your sample in to your TA.

Outside of regular laboratory hours, during this semester, we will attempt to extract DNA from your sample. If you would like to participate in this activity for extra credit, please let your instructor know. The Gentra Systems™ protocol we will use is as follows.

Purgene™ DNA Collection from Buccal Cell

Cell Lysis

Scrape inside of mouth using 10 strokes with a sterile nylon bristle cytology brush. (This is what you've done today!) Remove collection brush from handle using a sterile scissors or razor blade and place into 1.5 ml centrifuge tube containing 300 µl **Cell Lysis Solution.**

Incubate sample at 65°C for 15–60 minutes, or, if maximum yield is required, add 1.5 µl **Proteinase K Solution** (20 mg/ml) to the cell lysate, mix by inverting 25 times, and incubate at 55°C for 1 hour to overnight. Samples are stable in **Cell Lysis Solution** for at least 2 years at room temperature.

Remove brush from **Cell Lysis Solution**, scraping the brush on the sides of the tube to facilitate removal of lysate from the collection brush head. The brush head can be left in the **Cell Lysis Solution** for sample transport. However, the brush head should be removed for long-term storage.

RNase Treatment (Optional)

1. Add 1.5 µl **RNase A Solution** to the cell lysate.
2. Mix the sample by inverting the tube 25 times and incubate at 37°C for 15 minutes.

Protein Precipitation

1. Cool sample to room temperature by placing on ice for 1 minute.
2. Add 100 µl **Protein Precipitation Solution** to the RNase A-treated cell lysate. Vortex vigorously at high speed for 20 seconds to mix the **Protein Precipitation Solution** uniformly with the cell lysate.
3. Place tube in an ice bath for 5 minutes.
4. Centrifuge at 13,000–16,000 × g for 3 minutes. The precipitated proteins should form a tight, white pellet.

DNA Precipitation

1. Pour the supernatant containing the DNA (leaving behind the precipitated protein pellet) into a clean 1.5 ml microfuge tube containing 300 µl **100% Isopropanol** (2propanol) and 0.5 µl **Gentra Glycogen Solution** (20 mg/ml).
2. Mix the tube by inverting gently 50 times and keep tube at room temperature for at least 5 minutes.
3. Centrifuge at 13,000–16,000 × g for 5 minutes. The DNA may or may not be visible as a small white pellet, depending on yield.
4. Pour off supernatant and drain tube on clean absorbent paper. Add 300 µl **70% Ethanol** and invert tube several times to wash the DNA pellet.
5. Centrifuge at 13,000–16,000 × g for 1 minute. Carefully pour off the ethanol. *Pellet may be loose so pour slowly and watch pellet.* Invert and drain the tube on clean absorbent paper and allow to air dry 10–15 minutes.

DNA Hydration

1. Add 20 µl **DNA Hydration Solution** (20 µl will give a concentration of 50 ng/µl if the yield is 1 µg DNA).
2. Rehydrate DNA by incubating sample 1 hour at 65°C and/or overnight at room temperature. If possible, tap tube periodically to aid in dispersing the DNA. Store DNA at 4°C. For long-term storage, store at –20°C or –80°C.

LAB

2

Physiological Anthropology

OBJECTIVES

- Metabolic indicators of disease: human variation in the composition of urine
- Cell division and mutation basics
- Cultural/Environmental filters influencing gene expression
- PKU and melanin abnormalities; karyotyping

Traditionally, physiological anthropology has explored the biochemical and physiological levels of human biodiversity in an effort to understand the underlying biological and non-biological (e.g., cultural) forces that promote and maintain certain patterns of variation in contemporary humans. In this lab you will investigate the metabolic abnormalities underlying traits of known inheritance such as PKU whose phenotypic expression is influenced by environmental factors. This lab also presents material on karyotyping and an experiment on variation in the chemical constituents of human biological fluids.

Purpose of This Laboratory

Human biochemical variation is extensive, even though we are all members of the same genus, species, and subspecies. Understanding variation at the physiological level helps us appreciate how our ancestors have been able to adapt to so many different environments. This laboratory takes one common metabolic by-product, urine, and gives you an opportunity to evaluate biochemical variation in it and some of the physiological implications of this variation. Study the cultural/environmental filters diagram so that you can appreciate how gene expression can be altered by nongenetic forces. Can you think of specific examples? Consider how karyotypes are made. Remember that under normal conditions, the chromosomes are not neatly lined up as in the final photographs! The exercises on PKU and melanin abnormalities should help you understand how genetically based metabolic alterations can influence the phenotype. Look up additional information on PKU on the Internet to supplement your understanding.

Goals and Objectives

By the end of the lab, you should understand the concept of modern human physiological variation and some of the methods used to measure and analyze that variation. The purpose of this lab is to investigate the range of variation in biochemical traits of presumed simple inheritance. There are four main laboratory activities:

1. Conduct an analysis of components of human biological fluids and identify variation in these constituents.
2. Discuss the various kinds of mutation and their impact on gene expression.
3. Review normal and abnormal human karyotypes and complete the exercises provided.
4. Discuss the relationship of the genotype to the phenotype using the example of PKU (phenylketonuria). Evaluate the relationship of this metabolic abnormality to melanin production and albinism.

Key Terms and Topics

glucose, bilirubin, ketone, specific gravity, blood, pH, protein, urobilinogen, nitrite, leukocytes, in vitro diagnosis, urinalysis, Klinefelter's syndrome, Trisomy 21, XYY phenotypes, karyotypes, PKU (phenylketonuria), melanin, albinism, natural selection, biochemical individuality

Pre-Lab Assignments

(due at the beginning of the lab)

1. Keep a record of the foods and drinks that you consume for 2 days before your lab. Collect a mid-stream urine sample (your own or someone else's) just before your lab in the container provided and bring it to lab with you. Only you will be handling your own urine. The unknown biological samples are sterile.

2. Read the background information on phenylketonuria included in this lab as well as the mitosis and meiosis handout given in lecture.

Laboratory Activities

Laboratory Activity 1. Experimental analysis of human urine (artificial and natural)

During this exercise, you will test *in vitro* your own and unknown samples of artificial urine for glucose, bilirubin, ketone, specific gravity, blood, pH, protein, urobilinogen, nitrite, and leukocytes. You will be provided all necessary supplies and instructions by your TA. Follow the procedures and compare your individual results with the values you obtain for the unknown samples.

Materials for This Experiment

- Latex gloves
- Timer
- 5 Multistix 10 SG reagent strips for urinalysis
- Test tubes with unknown and self sample
- Urine collection kit

Place approximately 5 cc of your self sample into the empty test tube and return this test tube to the rack. Discard any excess urine sample in the toilets across from the lab.

Initialize your timer and begin testing sample 1 using a single reagent strip. Carefully remove the strip after the appropriate times and note the results (compare against the standard colors in the reference chart). Continue the analyses of samples 2–5 using a new reagent strip for each sample. Record your results on the following table:

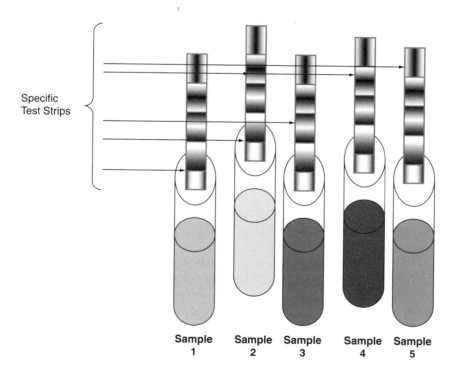

Specific Test Strips

Sample 1   Sample 2   Sample 3   Sample 4   Sample 5

Data Form for Results of Experimental Analysis of Artificial and Natural Urine

	Sample 1	Sample 2	Sample 3	Sample 4	Sample 5
Glucose					
Bilirubin					
Ketone					
Specific Gravity					
Blood					
pH					
Protein					
Urobilinogen					
Nitrite					
Leukocytes					

Additional comments on experiment: _____

_____

_____

_____

Lab Activity 2. Discussion of cell division and mutation

Discuss the processes of mitosis and meiosis and the functional consequences of each for the mammalian cell. Discuss the various kinds of mutation and be able to give practical examples of each.

Mutation as a Source of Genetic Variation in Proteins

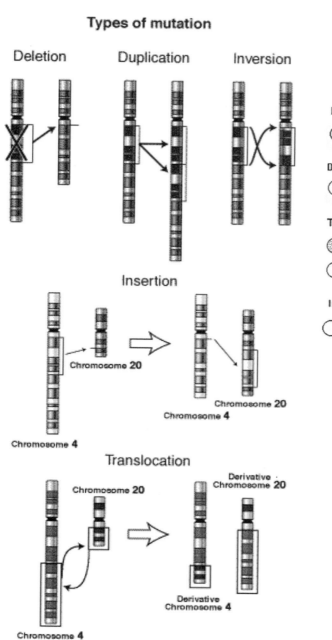

Types of mutation

Deletion   Duplication   Inversion

Insertion

Chromosome 20

Chromosome 20
Chromosome 4

Chromosome 4

Translocation

Chromosome 20

Derivative Chromosome 20

Derivative Chromosome 4

Chromosome 4

Mutations produce variations in the sequence of codons in a gene or in the sequence or genes on a chromosome. The various types of mutation are depicted in the diagrams to your left and below.

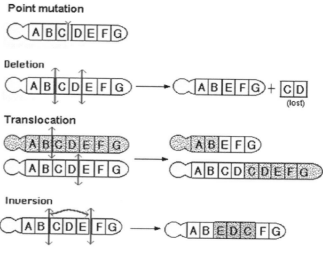

Point mutation

A B C D E F G

Deletion

A B C D E F G → A B E F G + C D (lost)

Translocation

A B C D E F G   →   A B E F G

A B C D E F G   A B C D C D E F G

Inversion

A B C D E F G → A B E D C F G

Mutations of Chromosomes

Lab Activity 3. Discussion of cultural/environmental filters influencing gene expression

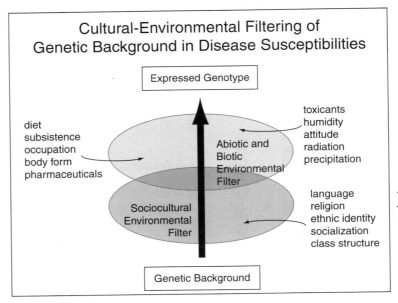

Cultural-Environmental Filtering of Genetic Background in Disease Susceptibilities

Jackson, 2003. *J. Child Health* 1(3):369–86.

This diagram depicts how genetic background is modified as the genetic information is exposed to various filters. The result is the expressed genotype or phenotype, which, as a result of these cultural-environmental modifications, is not an exact reflection of the genetic "blueprint."

Review the above diagram and be prepared to discuss the implications of the diagram for understanding the relationship between genetic background and expressed genotype (= phenotype) under various conditions. Consider possible examples of specific modifying variables.

Examples of Specific Filtering Agents:

Diet:	Genetic Background:	Phenotype Produced:
Wheat and barley	susceptibility to celiac disease	celiac disease

Pharmaceuticals:	Genetic Background:	Phenotype Produced:
Chloramphenicol	MTDNA 16srRNA	drug resistance to this antibiotic

Lab Activity 4: Other human metabolic diversity: discussion of PKU genetics, phenotypes, and melanin production

Read the background information provided below and then complete the three Punnet Squares exercises in lab.

QUESTION: If only one parent is a silent carrier of the gene for PKU, what is the probability that an off-spring will have the disease? *PKU is recessive. There is a 0% chance that the offspring will carry the disease because none of the children are homozygous recessive*

% express = 0%
% carriers = 50%

Review the (simplified) biochemical pathway for melanin production.

QUESTION: When can albinism occur? *— If you do not have tyrosine, than this will cause you not to have melanin causing albinism.*

QUESTION: What is the relationship between PKU and melanin production? (HINT: Why do many individuals with PKU also have light hair color?) *People w/ PKU do not produce melanin. They have light hair b/c they don't have eu... and pheo... and the reason they don't have eu... and pheo... is b/c they require tyrosine and melanin is produced from tyrosine.*

can be controlled through diet construction

Background Information

PKU (phenylketonuria) was first discovered in 1934. It is a rare, inherited metabolic disease that when untreated produces mental retardation and other neurological problems. When a very strict phenylalanine-restricted diet is begun early and well-maintained, affected children can develop normally and have a normal life span. PKU results from the absence of a single enzyme known as phenylalanine hydroxylase. This enzyme normally converts the essential amino acid, phenylalanine, to another amino acid, tyrosine. However, when a normal form of this enzyme is lacking, the phenylalanine builds up and is toxic to the central nervous system. PKU is associated with decreased IQ and other important neurological deficits although there is significant individual variation in the severity of PKU. Much of the variability in the metabolic expression of PKU is correlated with genetic diversity in the disorder. There are at least 105 different mutations known for the gene that causes PKU, although the version that causes mild PKU is the most common abnormal form.

NORMAL FEMALE KARYOTYPE

NORMAL MALE KARYOTYPE

PKU is transmitted via an autosomal recessive gene (known as PAH) located on chromosome 12 (CIRCLED). Autosomal recessive means that for a child to express this disease, both parents must be heterozygote "silent carriers" of the gene. When two such carriers produce a child, there is a 1 : 4 (or 25%) chance for each pregnancy that the baby will have PKU. The incidence of carriers in the general population is approximately 1 : 50 people, but the chance that two carriers will mate is only 1 : 2,500. PKU may be of Celtic origin as its highest frequencies are in Ireland (1 affected person per 4,500) and West Scotland. In the United States, the frequency of PKU is about 1 affected person per 8,000 among European-Americans and about 1 affected person per 50,000 among African Americans. Since children with PKU can have a favorable outcome when treated early and consistently and the majority of Americans are of European descent, all newborns are screened for this disorder in the United States.

Given the severe symptoms associated with PKU, what might account for the high frequency of this disorder, particularly among the Celts and their descendants? In 1986, Woolf suggested that there may be a heterozygous advantage in PKU which operates through protection against the toxic effects of ochratoxin A. This mycotoxin is produced by several species of *Aspergillus* and *Penicillium* infesting stored grains and other foods. The mild, wet climate of Ireland and West Scotland tends to encourage the growth of molds. Furthermore, these areas have suffered repeated famines during which moldy food was eaten. Heterozygous women ("silent carriers") appear to have a lower spontaneous abortion rate. Slightly higher levels of phenylalanine in the fetus may increase its chances of survival in the face of exposure to ochratoxin A, a known and common abortifacient (a factor that causes abortion).

Now, let's turn our attention to melanin. Melanin is the pigment commonly found in our skin, hair, and many of our internal organs (e.g., the brain). In human hair, for example, all the different hair colors are due to just two types of pigment (melanin) called eumelanins and pheomelanins. Eumelanins are the dark brown and black pigments while pheomelanins are the red and blonde pigments. The different colors of hair in different people are due to a combination of these two different basic biochemical structures. By mixing the two types together in different concentrations the many different shades of hair color are made.

Eumelanins are very strong, stable proteins made from tyrosine. The large eumelanin biochemical structure is formed by processing the amino acid tyrosine into dopa and dopamine and connecting together several of these molecules to form eumelanin. The key enzyme in this process is tyrosinase. The more tyrosinase activity the more eumelanin is formed. This is one method by which different people have different shades of brown to black hair color. More tyrosinase activity results in more pigment production and so initially we have a darker hair color in early adult life. As we get older, tyrosinase activity increases. It is most active in middle age and thereafter tyrosinase activity decreases, which is why our hair tends to lighten as we age. There are also other biochemical mechanisms by which the shade of hair color is regulated. Several factors interact with tyrosinase to help regulate eumelanin production. In addition, another key limiting factor in hair color is the availability of the raw tyrosine ingredient. A lack of tyrosine availability means the tyrosinase enzyme makes eumelanin at full capacity. From this you can now understand why many people with PKU have diluted melanogenesis (melanin formation) and lighter hair colors.

Pheomelanins are also made from the same tyrosine as eumelanins and the process is much the same with tyrosinase playing a key role. Pheomelanins are produced when an intermediate product in the eumelanin production pathway interacts with the amino acid cysteine. This results in the formation of a pheomelanin molecule that contains sulfur from the cysteine. These molecules are yellow to orange in color. So this is another way by which different shades of hair color can be produced. The more interaction there is between dopaquinone and cysteine the more yellow and orange pigments are produced.

Thus those people with darker hair have relatively more eumelanin production. People with true red hair produce more pheomelanin. In these cases, the pathway to eumelanin formation is largely inhibited. Because people with red hair are less able to make the dark eumelanin pigment their skin is generally quite pale and burns easily with sun exposure. A study that analyzed the amount of eumelanin and pheomelanin in human hair suggested that black hair contains approximately 99% eumelanin and 1% pheomelanin, brown and blond hair contain 95% eumelanin and 5% pheomelanin, and red hair contains 67% eumelanin and 33% pheomelanin (Borges, 2001). Although people with dark hair may still produce the yellow/orange pheomelanin, it is largely masked by the dark eumelanin pigment and we cannot see much of it. However, the red/yellow pheomelanin is believed to cause the warm, golden, or auburn tones found in some types of brown hair.

Reference: Borges, C. R., Roberts, J. C., Wilkins, D. G., & Rollins, D. E. 2001. Relationship of melanin degradation products to actual melanin content: Application to human hair. *Anal Biochem* (Mar 1) 290(1):116–25.

PKU and albinism

Complete the Punnett Squares exercises to better understand the inheritance and transmission of PKU from one generation to the next.

QUESTION: Since PKU affects melanin synthesis, which of the melanins is likely to be most affected by phenylketonuria? Why? *Eumelanins, use more tyrosine.*

QUESTION: Do you think that the current treatment for PKU, restriction of phenylalanine from the diet, would affect melanin synthesis? Why or why not?

PKU-related PUNNETT SQUARES Exercises

NOTE: The gene for PKU is known as PAH.

PATERNAL

	PAH normal	PAH abnormal
MATERNAL PAH normal		
MATERNAL PAH abnormal		

PATERNAL

	PAH abnormal	PAH abnormal
MATERNAL PAH normal		
MATERNAL PAH normal		

PATERNAL

	PAH normal	PAH normal
MATERNAL PAH abnormal		
MATERNAL PAH normal		

Simplified Biochemical Pathway for Melanin Production

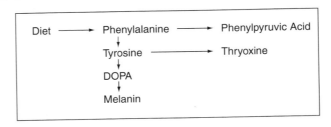

For individuals with PKU, discuss what happens when their diet includes significant quantities of the amino acid phenylalanine. Why is this phenylalanine transformed into phenylpyruvic acid rather than tyrosine? How does PKU affect DOPA and melanin production?

Lab Activity 5. Review of normal and abnormal karyotypes

A karyotype is a pictorial or photographic representation of all the metaphase chromosomes in an individual cell. Its main purpose is to detect abnormalities in chromosome number and morphology. Most of these abnormalities are associated with overt clinical defects. Read the background information and then complete the worksheets on karyotypes at the beginning of the next lab as homework.

Since the karyotype is species-specific, a wide range of number, size, and shape of metaphase chromosomes can be observed in eukaryotic (multicelled) organisms. Even closely related organisms may have quite different karyotypes. For example, humans (*Homo sapiens*) normally have 46 chromosomes while chimpanzees (*Pan troglodytes*) have 48 chromosomes. Quite distinct organisms may have similar numbers of chromosomes; for example, chimpanzees, potatoes (*Solanum tuberosum*), and tobacco (*Nicotiana tabacum*) all have 48 chromosomes; rats (*Rattus norvegicus*) and bread wheat (*Triticum aestivum*) each have 42 chromosomes.

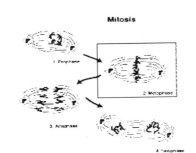

How is a karyotype made? First we must arrest cells in **metaphase.** We then stain the cells with a specific stain so that the chromosomes exhibit transverse bands that are specific for each pair of chromosomes. Then we photograph and cut out individual chromosomes from the photograph and paste them into place (so they are lined up nicely). Using a karyotype, chromosomes can be identified and categorized based on several characteristics:

1. Length—chromosomes can be ordered by size and numbered from the longest to the shortest.

2. Position of the centromere

3. Banding patterns found in chromosomes stained with various chemicals

   a. Dark banding patterns represent heterochromatic regions that are generally located near the ends of chromosomes or near the centromere.

   b. Light banding patterns represent euchromatic regions that undergo a cycle of contraction and extension.

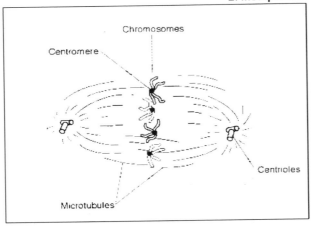

2. Metaphase

How do we identify chromosomes in humans? Here are some strategies:

1. Autosomes or non-sex chromosomes are numbered from 1–22 on the basis of length: 1 is the longest and 22 is the shortest.
2. Sex chromosomes are X and Y and are identified separately.
3. Each chromosome is divided into two arms: p and q.
4. Each arm is divided into regions (1, 2, 3, . . .).
5. Each region is then divided into bands.

The normal human male and female karyotypes are presented below. Also presented are several abnormal karyotypes. Can you identify the abnormalities associated with each? Complete this exercise for HOME-WORK and turn in at the beginning of Lab 3.

Autosomes and sex

Normal Human Male Karyotype

Normal Human Female Karyotype

Methods and Materials for Making Artificial Human Urine

The following reagents will be necessary for the preparation of normal human urine (Kark et al., 1964):

- Albumin powder (egg or bovine)
- Creatinine
- Distilled water
- Potassium chloride
- Sodium chloride
- Sodium phosphate (monobasic)
- Urea

A class of 30 students, working in groups of two, would require a class total of at least 1 liter of artificial urine for specific gravity and dipstick testing. The following instructions are for the preparation of approximately 2 liters of normal urine; half can be stored or used for abnormal urine studies.

To 1.5 liters of distilled water add 36.4 g of urea and mix until all the crystals are dissolved. Then add 15.0 g of sodium chloride, 9.0 g of potassium chloride, and 9.6 g of sodium phosphate; mix until the solution is clear. Check the pH with indicator paper or a pH meter to ensure the pH is within the 5 to 7 pH range for normal urine; if the solution is out of this pH range the pH may be lowered with 1N hydrochloric acid or raised with 1N sodium hydroxide.

Next, place a urine hydrometer into the solution and dilute with water until the solution is within the specific gravity range of 1.015 to 1.025. This solution will serve as the storage stock solution of "normal urine solution" and may be kept refrigerated for several weeks or frozen in plastic containers for months. Before use, the stock solution should be warmed to room temperature. Then, to ensure a similarity to human urine, 4.0 g of creatinine and 100 mg of albumin may be slowly mixed into the 2 liters of the so-called normal urine solution.

Abnormal Human Urine

The artificial normal human urine may be modified to mimic several diseased or periodic conditions that are detectable in the urine. Abnormal urine is normally not available from student samples, thus students rarely experience the test results associated with disease. Also, the artificial abnormal urine is an excellent medium to test student skills and observations with the clinical testing of urine. The following conditions may be exhibited by using the "normal urine solution" and additional inexpensive reagents.

1. **Glycosuria:** High levels of glucose due to diabetes mellitus, pregnancy, excessive stress, renal tubular damage, and brain damage. Add a minimum of 600 mg of glucose (dextrose) to each liter of "normal urine solution" to obtain a minimally detectable level of glycosuria. A moderate to high level of glycosuria can be achieved by adding 2.5 to 5.0 g of glucose to each liter of the solution. Sucrose or other sugars will not substitute for glucose; only glucose yields positive results with most urine test strips. Vitamin C (ascorbic acid) contamination of the urine, at values of 400 mg/l or greater, though, does yield false positive glucose results. This may add an interesting twist to the study of the accuracy and limitations of urinalysis.

2. **Proteinuria:** A high level of protein in the urine is an excellent indicator of glomerular damage. In the absence of glomerular damage, elevated urine protein may result from excessive exercise, cold exposure, and acute abdominal diseases. Protein levels in excess of 300 mg of albumin per liter or "normal urine solution" will give positive results. Severe renal damage may be exemplified by adding 1 g of albumin to each liter of the urine solution.

3. **Ketonuria:** Ketones of various types, which are normal liver metabolites, should not be found in detectable amounts in the urine. Elevated ketone levels are indicative of cold exposure, diabetes mellitus, dietary imbalances, and genetically or chemically acquired metabolic abnormalities. Ketonuria may be exhibited by adding a minimum of 100 mg of acetoacetic acid or at least 1 ml of acetone to 1 liter of "normal urine solution."

4. **Urine pH imbalances:** Acidic urine can be obtained by adjusting the pH of the "normal urine solution" to a pH of 4.0 to 4.5 with 1N HCl. Consistent acidic urine is a sign of metabolic or respiratory acidosis, methanol poisoning, or metabolic disorders (e.g., phenylketonuria). Alkaline urine is obtained by adjusting the pH of the "normal urine solution" to a pH of 8 to 9 using 1N NaOH. Consistent alkaline urine is indicative of metabolic and respiratory alkalosis and urinary tract infections.

5. **Hyposthenuria:** Urine should have a specific gravity range of 1.015 to 1.025; some daily variation outside of this range is normal. Consistent production of dilute urine, with a specific gravity less that 1.015, is an indication of cardiovascular problems, diabetes insipidus, or renal tubule problems. The specific gravity of "normal urine solution" may be lowered by adding distilled water to a volume of the stock solution until the specific gravity approaches 1.005.

6. **Hemoglobinuria:** Hemoglobin in the urine results from excess levels of free hemoglobin in the blood due to excessive red blood cell lysis, renal damage, or the normal menstrual flow. Bovine (cow) hemoglobin is an inexpensive powdered reagent available from many biological and chemical supply companies. Hemoglobinuria can be exhibited by adding 260 mg of bovine hemoglobin to 1 liter of "normal urine solution." Hematuria, or the presence of whole blood in urine (a good indication of glomerular damage), may be modeled using heparinized or defibrinated sheep blood normally used in microbiological and cell cultures. The urine test strips are normally sensitive to 1 ml of whole blood in 1 liter of urine solution.

7. **Leukocyte presence:** This is a difficult test and requires the use of small amounts of reagent and urine. The presence of leukocytes in urine indicates urinary tract damage or infection. The urine test strips can be faked into giving a positive leukocyte response by the addition of enzymes called esterases. Esterases are available through biological, chemical and histological supply companies. Esterase activity is measured in activity units; many companies sell the enzymes by the unit or by units per mass. A positive test for leukocytes may be achieved by adding 100 to 200 units of pork or rabbit liver esterase to 100 ml of the "normal urine solution." The leukocyte test must be performed immediately after the addition of the enzyme and may be performed on 10 ml samples in small test tubes.

A whole spectrum of urine abnormalities could be included in one sample by mixing the appropriate amounts of the "abnormal conditions reagents" into a common 1 liter volume of the "normal urine solution." For example, the urine from a patient with diabetes mellitus would have urine that tests positive for glycosuria and ketonuria, while a patient with glomerular damage would have urine that is positive for proteinuria, hemoglobinuria, and hematuria.

The above method for the production of artificial urine is pragmatic for several reasons. It allows students to perform urinalysis without the fear of contamination by hazardous microorganisms. The procedure allows for the manipulation of the "urine" so students can encounter the diseased urine types not normally found among student urine samples. The materials for making the artificial urine are inexpensive and available from many biological and chemical supply companies. Lastly, the preparation is simple, and large quantities may be stored for several months. The artificial urine is only accurate for use with urine test strips or related reagents: it is not intended for use with electronic clinical analyzers.

LAB

3

Modeling Microevolution

O B J E C T I V E S

- Population biology and evolutionary change
- Habitat change and altered survival games
- Interpreting human microevolutionary scenarios

The environment continues to modify our genetics by influencing who survives, reproduces, and passes on their genes to the next generation. How much of contemporary and ancient human population variation is a reflection of past or present geographical differences in specific evolutionary forces? In this lab students will explore the effect of habitat change on survival using three different habitat simulation models. This lab also devotes considerable attention to the evolutionary interpretation of various plausible anthropological scenarios.

Purpose of This Laboratory

Often in biological anthropology we use simplified models of natural events to better understand the effects of evolutionary processes. In this laboratory you will replicate such processes as natural selection, genetic drift, and gene flow in hypothetical populations so as to better understand how these same processes might proceed in real groups. As you do the exercises in this lab, try to imagine how these same events might manifest themselves in real human populations. Use your critical thinking skills to augment the labs, especially the scenarios. Remember that evolution is occurring all around us!

Goals and Objectives

The goal of this lab is to expand the knowledge of genetics you've gained at the molecular, cellular, and chromosomal levels to now make population-level assessments. The lab is divided into two parts. In the first part, you are expected to demonstrate, through a series of simulation exercises, the evolutionary effects of a changing habitat on individual and group survival and reproduction. In the second part of the lab, you will critique a set of five scenarios to understand the effects of different circumstances (some directed, some "random") on the gene pool of a population.

Key Terms and Topics

deme, meme, Hardy-Weinberg equilibrium, inbreeding, assertive mating, genetic drift, microevolution, macroevolution, effective population size, carrying capacity, glacial period, interglacial period, predation, infectious disease, stochastic vs. directed evolution

Pre-Lab Assignments

(due at the beginning of this lab)

1. Know the meanings of each of the key terms and topics for this lab.

2. Review the protocols for reenacting the microevolutionary events you will simulate using inanimate objects, so that you can get the most out of this exercise.

3. Be familiar with world geography and climatic diversity in various parts of the human range.

4. Go over the scenarios that you will contemplate in lab and research some background information on each.

5. Consider the effects of global warming on changing environmental selective pressures.

Laboratory Activities

Laboratory Activity 1. Evaluation of evolutionary effects of changing habitat on clan size, number, and distribution (aspects of survival value or biological fitness)

In this exercise, students will work in teams to illustrate how three sets of common ecological events:

a. predation,

b. desiccation and aridity in cold environments (associated with ice age conditions), and

c. interglacial period (including increased humidity, increased ambient temperatures, and increased infectious disease)

can serve as agents of natural selection. Students are divided into three groups. Each group will start with ten different clans, represented by ten different types of seeds. Three habitat boards that represent the three environmental conditions are provided. The habitat scenarios will "change" (by changing the conditions on the individual boards) due to one or more of the prescribed ecological events, predation or selective survival will occur, and susceptible members of the clans will be culled. The surviving individuals will reproduce and pass on the selected traits in the new environment.

Each group should perform all three habitat simulations and record and analyze the results (pre- and post-selection).

Here are the habitats you and your fellow students will be working in with your clans through several generations of exposure:

Habitat One

This environment has variable terrain and numerous predators. Predators routinely prey upon clan members, based upon visual identification of potential targets.

Habitat Two

This environment is undergoing desiccation as an ice age envelops the area. Under conditions of increasing aridity, the amount of habitable land is diminishing.

Habitat Three

This environment is in the middle of an interglacial period. With increasing temperatures and humidity, insect vectors, bacteria, molds, fungi, and viruses proliferate and infectious diseases target susceptible individuals and groups.

Clan Names for Habitat Change Game and Representative Seeds

1. Bhanja (Great Northern seeds)
2. Rocio (Black-eyed Pea seeds)
3. Orungo (Chick Pea seeds)
4. Sagiyama (Yellow Corn seeds)
5. Koutango (Lentil seeds)
6. Geta (Pinto Bean seeds)
7. Zinga (Brown Bean seeds)
8. Tonate (Kidney Bean seeds)
9. Powassan (Sunflower seeds)
10. Mucambo (Black Bean seeds)

Simulate Habitat Change

- Desiccation, aridity, ice age conditions
- Interglacial period, increased humidity, increased ambient temperatures, increased infectious disease
- Predation

Develop a Set of Assumptions about Each Clan

1. High homogeneity within each clan
2. High heterogeneity between clans
3. Seed morphology influences clan survival under conditions of habitat change

Here is how to "play" the habitat change game:

CLANS

ASSUMPTIONS	1	2	3	4	5	6	7	8	9	10
1.										
2.										
3.										

For Habitat One

1. Divide your group into the following subunits:
   a. *Guardians of the Clans* (jobs: disperse clan members, count surviving clan numbers after predation event, control clan reproduction).
   b. *Predators on the Clans* (jobs: prey on clan members, remove predators between predation episodes, keep track of predator "deaths" [e.g., if a predator rolls into a lake or fails to eat a clan member during a predation episode]).
   c. *Recorders of Clan Microevolution* (jobs: document changes in clan composition before and after predation, calculate overall change in population after three predation and reproduction events).

2. Disperse your "clan members" (individual seeds) throughout habitat one. You can disperse them randomly or according to a predesigned model. The Guardians of the Clans should decide.

3. Decide what kind of predators you have. The Predators on the Clans should decide.

4. Disperse your predators, based upon their identity, and physically remove from the habitat the clan members that are touched by the predators.

5. If you decide that your predators are birds, perhaps you want to drop the marbles from the sky above the habitat. If you decide that your predators are social carnivores, perhaps you will want to "roll" them into the habitat.

6. Between predation episodes, allow surviving clan members to reproduce themselves. One surviving clan member "self-generates" one new clan member. "Reproduction" means toss into the habitat another seed of the same clan.

7. Recorders of Clan Microevolution must keep track of the changes in the clan composition before and after predation, record these results systematically, take note of the clan's experiences in habitat one, and give an oral report to the lab as a whole on behalf of the group.

For Habitat Two

1. Divide your group into the following subunits:
   a. *Guardians of the Clans* (jobs: disperse clan members, count surviving clan numbers after glacial or interglacial event, control clan reproduction).
   b. *Keepers of the Ice* (jobs: "declare" either a glacial period or an interglacial period and expand or contract environmental "ice" accordingly).
   c. *Recorders of Clan Microevolution* (jobs: document changes in clan composition before and after changes in extent of environmental ice, calculate overall change in population after three glacial and interglacial periods and reproduction events).

2. Disperse your "clan members" (individual seeds) throughout habitat two. You can disperse them randomly or according to a predesigned model. The Guardians of the Clans should decide.

3. Decide what the initial weather conditions are for the clans. The Keepers of the Ice should decide.

4. Expand or constrict the ice, and physically remove from the habitat the clan members that are touched by the ice.

5. Keepers of the Ice should alternate between glacial and interglacial periods without regard to where the clans are dispersed.

6. Between glacial or interglacial episodes, allow surviving clan members to reproduce themselves. One surviving clan member "self-generates" one new clan member. "Reproduction" means toss into the habitat another seed of the same clan.

7. Recorders of Clan Microevolution must keep track of the changes in the clan composition before and after an ice event, record these results systematically, take note of the clan's experiences in habitat two, and give an oral report to the lab as a whole on behalf of the group.

For Habitat Three

1. Divide your group into the following subunits:

   a. *Guardians of the Clans* (jobs: disperse clan members, count surviving clan numbers after predation event, control clan reproduction).

   b. *Disease in the Clans* (jobs: attack clan members causing disease, remove infectious agents, between disease episodes, keep track of infectious agent "deaths" [e.g., if a infectious disease agent fails to make contact with a clan member during a disease episode]).

   c. *Recorders of Clan Microevolution* (jobs: document changes in clan composition before and after disease event, calculate overall change in population after three disease episodes and reproduction events).

2. Disperse your "clan members" (individual seeds) throughout habitat three. You can disperse them randomly or according to a predesigned model. The Guardians of the Clans should decide.

3. Decide what kind of infectious disease agents you have. The Disease in the Clans should decide.

4. Disperse your infectious disease agents, based upon their identity, and physically remove from the habitat the clan members that are touched by the disease agents.

5. If you decide that your disease agents are transmitted by flying insects (e.g., malaria), perhaps you want to throw the beads horizontally from the air just above the habitat. If you decide that insects that live on the land carry your infectious disease agents, perhaps you will want to "roll" them into the habitat.

6. Between disease episodes, allow surviving clan members to reproduce themselves. One surviving clan member "self-generates" one new clan member. "Reproduction" means toss into the habitat another seed of the same clan.

7. Recorders of Clan Microevolution must keep track of the changes in the clan composition before and after disease, record these results systematically, take note of the clan's experiences in habitat three, and give an oral report to the lab as a whole on behalf of the group.

Habitat Change Game

Data Sheet

Habitat _____

Clans and Seed Keys:

Bhanja = Great Northern
Sagiyama = Yellow Corn
Zinga = Brown Bean
Mucambo = Black Bean

Rocio = Black-eyed Pea
Koutango = Lentil
Tonato = Kidney Bean

Orungo = Chick Pea
Geta = Pinto Bean
Powassan = Sunflower Seed

	Bhanja	Rocio	Orungo	Sagiyama	Koutango	Geta	Zinga	Tonato	Powassan	Mucambo	Total
Generation #1 # deceased											
# survivors											
#offspring (survivors × 2)											
Generation #2 (survivors + offspring)											
# deceased											
# survivors											
# offspring (survivors × 2)											
Generation #3 (survivors + offspring)											

Habitat Change Game

Data Sheet

Habitat _____

Clans and Seed Keys:

Bhanja = Great Northern
Sagiyama = Yellow Corn
Zinga = Brown Bean
Mucambo = Black Bean

Rocio = Black-eyed Pea
Koutango = Lentil
Tonato = Kidney Bean

Orungo = Chick Pea
Geta = Pinto Bean
Powassan = Sunflower Seed

	Bhanja	Rocio	Orungo	Sagiyama	Koutango	Geta	Zinga	Tonato	Powassan	Mucambo	Total
Generation #1 # deceased											
# survivors											
#offspring (survivors × 2)											
Generation #2 (survivors + offspring)											
# deceased											
# survivors											
# offspring (survivors × 2)											
Generation #3 (survivors + offspring)											

Habitat Change Game

Habitat _____

Clans and Seed Keys:

Clan	Seed	Clan	Seed
Bhanja = Great Northern		Rocio = Black-eyed Pea	
Sagiyama = Yellow Corn		Koutango = Lentil	
Zinga = Brown Bean		Tonato = Kidney Bean	
Mucambo = Black Bean		Orungo = Chick Pea	
		Geta = Pinto Bean	
		Powassan = Sunflower Seed	

Data Sheet

	Bhanja	Rocio	Orungo	Sagiyama	Koutango	Geta	Zinga	Tonato	Powassan	Mucambo	Total
Generation #1 # deceased											
# survivors											
#offspring (survivors × 2)											
Generation #2 (survivors + offspring)											
# deceased											
# survivors											
# offspring (survivors × 2)											
Generation #3 (survivors + offspring)											

Lab Activity 2. Deconstructing gene-environment interactions: scenario/assessment evaluation

In this part of the lab, students will divide into roughly six discussion groups. Each group should discuss each of the five elaborated scenarios presented below. For each of the scenarios, your group should study and analyze the data presented and discuss the posed questions as well as any other questions that come up during the course of discussion. Each student should document the results of these discussions. Plan on discussing each scenario for at least 5 minutes. Be sure to document your discussions since some of the lab time will be devoted to a consideration of each of the scenarios and their human population genetic implications. Use these scenarios to better understand the real-life implications of such population genetic mechanisms as gene flow, genetic drift, assortive mating, natural selection, etc.

Scenario 1: "**Phenotypic and genotypic effects of introducing lactose-containing foods into the diets of lactose-intolerant groups**" Answer the three questions posed at the end of the scenario and discuss any additional issues concerning the relationship of genetic dominance, genetic recessiveness, and population frequency.

Scenario 2: "**Genetic effects of drift and inbreeding in a religious isolate**" Determine the probability of genotypes for each family. What are the predicted phenotypes of the offspring for each family? What are the group-level ramifications of certain frequencies?

Scenario 3: "**Genetic effects of migration and gene flow on the frequency of a marker gene**" Using words or diagrams, explain the effect of gene flow on the frequency of the *Fy-* (Duffy negative) gene in the Tuareg population over time.

Scenario 4: "**Selection in an urban group**" Answer the four questions posed at the end of the scenario.

Scenario 5: "**Reconstructing the pedigree of color blindness in a family**" Using the pedigree format provided, draw Maria's most probable ancestry. Explain the three statements cited in the scenario, using Punnett squares where appropriate.

Here are the texts of the scenarios:

1. **Phenotypic and Genotypic Effects of Introducing Lactose-Containing Foods into the Diets of Lactose-Intolerant Groups**

   Most mammals (including humans) do not consume milk beyond the weaning stage and are metabolically intolerant of lactose, the sugar in milk. This phenotype is considered the norm or "wild type." A handful of human groups (and a few animals such as the California sea lion) continue to produce lactase (the enzyme that breaks down lactose) well into adulthood. Most of the human groups that maintain high frequencies of this condition are northern Europeans. The current patterns of world cultural (and economic) dominance have spread many of the biocultural patterns of these groups to previously non-milk consuming groups. However, for individuals lacking adequate levels of lactase and exposed to high levels of lactose within a short time, the symptoms of lactose intolerance are often produced.

   As part of the American Dairy Council's Outreach Program to find new markets for milk-based products, a large gathering of Pima Native Americans is provided with unlimited supplies of free ice cream throughout their weeklong annual corn festival. Although many of the tribal elders are reluctant to consume the icy cones, Pima children and young adults like the sweet taste and smooth texture and lick cone after cone with unrestrained enthusiasm. Over the following two weeks, outbreaks of diarrhea, flatulence, constipation, and stomach pain affect nearly 95% of the Pima children and young adults of three villages.

   Assuming that these symptoms were due exclusively to the consumption of ice cream, how do these phenotypic effects compare with those that would have been expected among Danish children and young adults (nearly 100% tolerant) or among African America children and young adults (only 10% tolerant)? As noted above, genotypically, lactose intolerance appears to be a recessive condition yet it is the most common phenotype among humans. Provide an explanation as to how this can occur. In a group of 100 Pima children and young adults, what are the possible genotypes of the approximately five individuals who did not become ill after eating ice cream? Show all your work in your answers.

2. **Genetic Effects of Drift and Inbreeding in a Religious Isolate**

In an effort to increase the Jewish population in Palestine, the Government of Israel underwrites the relocation expenses of a group of 10,000 Askenazi Jews from a small enclave outside of Kiev, Russia, to the Middle East. This religious isolate was originally founded by two families and over many generations of living in Central and Eastern Europe, they have largely practiced endogamy (in-group marriage and reproduction). Now, certain genes appear to be concentrated in this group.

Among the group of migrants, 20% are homozygous for a gene (c_1) that causes a rare and nonlethal neurological impairment. The expression of this recessive gene results in slight mental disorientation and eye twitching at the onset of puberty. Scientists suspect that the gene's phenotypic expression may be linked to the hormonal shifts associated with adolescence. The normal gene is designated C.

Among the parents of the three nuclear families presented below, calculate the genotypic ratios for C and c_1. What are the phenotypic ratios among these families?
Rabin Family: David CC and Sarah Cc_1
Levitan Family: Hayim CC and Miriam c_1c_1
Halevy Family: Efram c_1c_1 and Rebekkah Cc_1

3. **Genetic Effects of Migration and Gene Flow on the Frequency of a Marker Gene**

In the mid-1960s a group of professional accountants from the United States was headed for an international conference on finance in Timbuktu, Mali, when their chartered plane became lost in an unexpected Saharan sandstorm. The pilot made an emergency landing 125 miles from Néma, Mauritania, and the 12 survivors struggled to reach the closest oasis town. For two months the combined efforts of the Malian, Mauritanian, and Senegalese air forces were unsuccessful in locating either the downed plane or the surviving accountants. U.S. Army Rangers are flown in but they too are unsuccessful in finding the missing accountants. After six months and no contact with the crash victims, search efforts were abandoned. On the ground, however, a group of nomadic Tuareg intercepted the wandering survivors within a few days of their crash landing and integrated them into their band.

After 30 years, all of the surviving female accountants (6 women) have been married to Tuareg men and about half of the surviving male accountants (3 men) are married to Tuareg women. Each union has produced at least three children and two grandchildren. Their children and grandchildren are raised as Tuareg and know nothing of the United States or professional finance. By chance, all of the surviving accountants carried a marker gene (Fy-) that was previously unknown among the Tuareg. Using one or more diagrams, depict how the frequency for the Fy- gene has been affected over time among the Tuareg as a result of gene flow from the surviving accountants and their descendants. Show all your work.

4. **Selection in an Urban Group**

In particular urban communities, tallness has been culturally favored for the last 150 years. During this time period, the majority of group heroes have been tall. Tall people are assumed to be the smartest, most talented, and most beautiful. Tall people have earned the most money, regardless of ability, have consistently received the best job offers, and have had the best opportunity to marry and reproduce. Most of the material products in these communities are made with tall people in mind and the value of tallness is constantly projected in the media. Special academic and professional opportunities are regularly made available for tall people so that their favored position is likely to be maintained throughout several future generations. It's tough being short because to be short is considered the antithesis of everything great that tallness represents. Yet, in spite of this clear bias, at least 1/3 of the population in these communities is short in stature.

Fifteen years ago, the growth enhancing properties of a certain soft drink become evident. If children with short parents could drink enough of the soft drink, they would be as tall as the children born of tall parents. The soft drink company began to make billions of dollars by promoting the growth enhancing effects of their product. However, there were a few drawbacks. The growth-promoting compound was only found in the bottled version of the soft drink, not in the cans. Also, the compound was only effective on growing children. Once full adult stature had been attained, the compound did not work.

In order to maintain sales, the soft drink company advertised that the growth-promoting compound was in both bottled and canned varieties of their soft drink and that it was effective at all age groups. To emphasize this point, they used tall adult models as spokespersons to promote the beverage.

What proportion of the short children can be expected to benefit from the growth enhancing compound and what proportion will remain unaffected if 80% of the soft drinks were canned and only 20% were bottled? How will the regular consumption of the compound begin to alter phenotypic frequencies? Can consumption affect genotypic frequencies? How will the proportion of short people be affected over time? Consider these questions in some detail.

5. **Reconstructing the Pedigree of Color Blindness in a Family**
   Señora Maria Rodriquez de Salazar is a carrier for the genes causing red/green color blindness. These X-linked conditions are inherited as recessive traits and code for a defective class of gene products known as opsins. In the hemizygous and homozygous conditions, this results in an inability to see red and green as distinct colors. Maria is the great granddaughter of a very famous family of Spanish dancers, Benito Cruz and Rosita Maldonado de Cruz. Benito was known to be red/green color blind and therefore must have been hemizygous for these genes. Rosita's genotype was unknown. Their daughter Magali (Maria's grandmother) was not known to be color blind. Magali's daughter was definitely not color blind and neither was Magali's first son Julio. However, Magali's son Andres (Maria's father) was color blind.

   Using the following standard format for pedigree analysis, indicate Maria's expected pedigree for the X-linked recessive inheritance pattern. Then explain briefly but clearly WHY the following statements are true:

1. All affected males pass sex-linked recessive genes to their daughters who normally become heterozygous carriers. These carriers pass the gene on to 50% of their sons.

2. Sex-linked recessive genes are never transmitted from father to son but can be transmitted from grandfathers to grandsons.

3. The phenotypic expression of sex-linked recessive genes is much more frequent in males than in females. Write clear responses to each of these points.

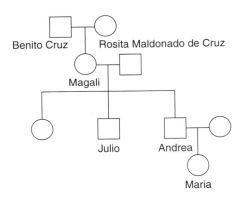

Lab Activity 3. Comparative gene frequency distributions

Compare the frequency distributions presented below and describe, using the best genetic terminology, how groups B, C, D, E, F, G, H, and I differ from group A. Each column represents the frequency of a particular allele in a specific group. Similarly shaded columns represent identical alleles. The distribution of alleles in population A represents the frequencies of five related variants of a gene at time 1. The distributions of alleles in populations B through I reflect the alleles present after various evolutionary events. Initially the distribution of alleles in populations B through I were identical to those in population A. So, evaluate each comparison and hypothesize what evolutionary forces may have been in operation. Work individually but discuss your results collectively.

Remember: DIRECTIONAL SELECTION is directed against one side of the distribution.
STABILIZING SELECTION is directed against the extreme ends of the distribution.
SPECIATING SELECTION is directed the distribution's mean.

EXAMPLE:

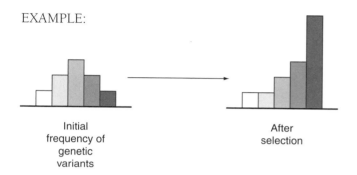

Initial frequency of genetic variants

After selection

Shift in gene frequency distribution? YES
Direction of shift? INCREASED FREQUENCY OF DARK GREY VARIANT
Likely evolutionary process in effect? NATURAL SELECTION: (It is due to directional selection against the white end of the distribution.)
Why? (be creative here) UV RADIATION EFFECTS

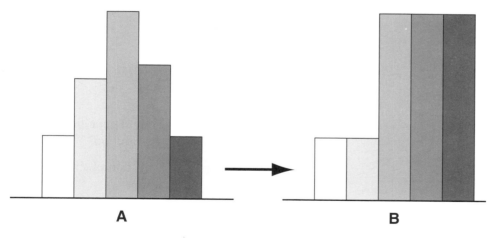

A

B

Shift in gene frequency distribution? Y N

Direction of shift?

Likely evolutionary process in effect?

Why? (i.e., what could cause this?)

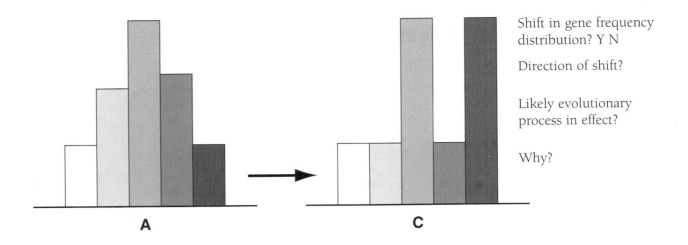

Shift in gene frequency
distribution? Y N

Direction of shift?

Likely evolutionary
process in effect?

Why?

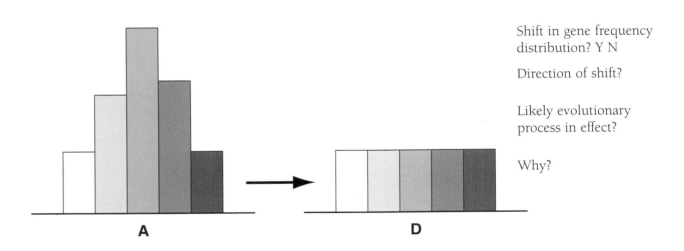

Shift in gene frequency
distribution? Y N

Direction of shift?

Likely evolutionary
process in effect?

Why?

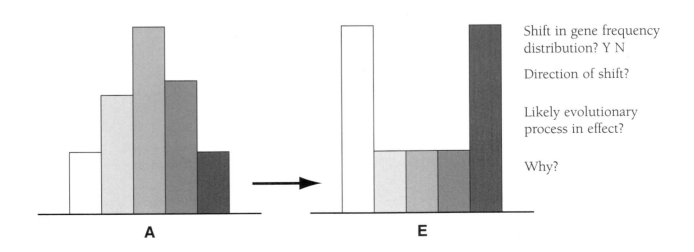

Shift in gene frequency
distribution? Y N

Direction of shift?

Likely evolutionary
process in effect?

Why?

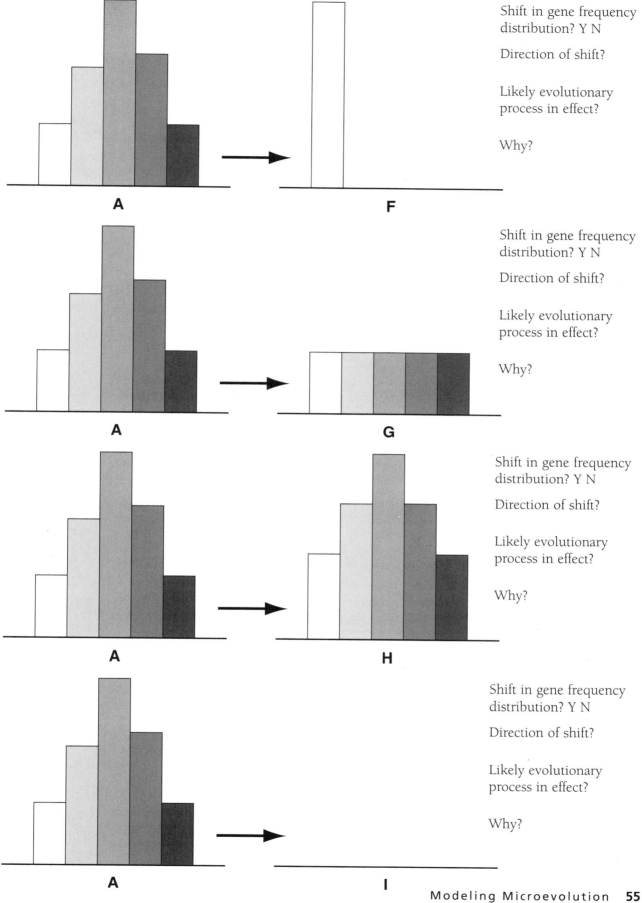

Shift in gene frequency
distribution? Y N

Direction of shift?

Likely evolutionary
process in effect?

Why?

Shift in gene frequency
distribution? Y N

Direction of shift?

Likely evolutionary
process in effect?

Why?

Shift in gene frequency
distribution? Y N

Direction of shift?

Likely evolutionary
process in effect?

Why?

Shift in gene frequency
distribution? Y N

Direction of shift?

Likely evolutionary
process in effect?

Why?

Post-Lab Assignments

Type a one-page, single-spaced assessment for each of the post-lab deconstruction scenarios presented below.

Deconstructing Scenarios

The purpose of this exercise is to identify various mechanisms of potential evolutionary significance in quasi-historical human multigenerational stories. Read each scenario carefully and note situations within which such mechanisms as natural selection, genetic drift, gene flow, and mutation may be influencing the population biology of the groups under consideration. Discuss your results fully in one-page essays (one essay per scenario) and justify your assertions. Include graphics depicting the changes in gene frequencies, if you like.

Scenario 1: 25,000 years B.P. (before present), a group of 50 northeast Asia men, women, and children has just succeeded in crossing a temporary land bridge near the current day Bering Straits. As they travel east and then southeast into modern-day Alaska, an unexpected blizzard disorients the group and they seek refuge in an isolated inland valley. Under conditions of extreme cold, they subsist entirely off of caribou. Stranded all winter, two elderly members of the group do not survive. The following spring, a zoonotic (= animal derived) epidemic kills all of the children and all but three of the women, all of whom are biological sisters. The children born to these three sisters over the next 25 years carry on the group's traditions including honoring the three sisters as the founding mothers of the new settlement. Over many generations, these three women become immortalized as goddesses and stories relating their survival in a new environment become a critical part of the group's spiritual beliefs. The three surviving sisters contributed both biological and cultural information of relevance to the next generation. Identify which major evolutionary processes have influenced the gene pool of this group and state why. Consider the impact of evolutionary processes (on individuals) on the dynamics of the group as a whole.

Scenario 2: The time is 500 years B.P. As the great Zulu nation pushes southward toward modern day Azania (South Africa), the Khoi and San speaking peoples (!Kung speakers) retreat into remote and nearly uninhabitable regions of the Kalahari Desert. Zulu raids into these regions and the subordination of the Khoi and San result in some Khoi and San women being incorporated into the large, militaristic Zulu nation. Most Khoi and San, however, prefer the protection of isolation and manage to survive in these ecologically very marginal areas. Subsequent to the southward expansion of the Bantu-speaking Zulu peoples, Europeans from the Netherlands and the British Isles arrive further squeezing the Khoi and San into areas where food is of limited quantity and quality. As Khoi and San lands are increasingly restricted, nearly all cultural Khoi and San are found living in the less desirable semi-arid regions of the area. Their main food here is a particular root known to have mutagenic properties. After generations of residence in these areas, the Khoi and San peoples become physically smaller; smaller individuals appear to disproportionately survive under these specific desert conditions. What kinds of evolutionary processes are in operation in these groups? Discuss population fluctuations, effects on gene frequencies, and within group diversity. Justify your answers.

LAB

4

Comparative Primate Anatomy

OBJECTIVES

- Skeletal identification and primate functional anatomy
- Comparative anthropometrics and anthroposcopics
- Calculation of human cranial capacity
- Assessment of hand dominance
- Mammalian brain weights and body weights
- Comparative dermatoglyphics

Anatomy is a branch of biology concerned with the study of body structure of various organisms, including humans. Anatomical assessments are part of the historical foundations of biological anthropology. These assessments can include measurements of the body, testing for different abilities, identification of anatomy-based preferences, and observations of morphological differences. Usually a biological anthropologist interested in this area has a specific trait in mind before starting to take measurements or make observations, and this trait has some research relevance. In this lab you will perform a variety of tasks to collect data on yourself and your classmates, and you will analyze the data and present it in a meaningful format. Since you will be making scientific measurements, you must use the metric system. All of the tools you will use are calibrated in centimeters (cm) and millimeters (mm). An inch is equal to 2.54 cm.

Purpose of This Laboratory

Understanding primate anatomy is a key part of biological anthropology and a foundation for traditional forensic research. Each anatomical part is associated with a set of particular functions, which you should learn in conjunction to the identification of the bones. In this laboratory you are expected to learn the major parts of the primate skeleton and the functional equivalents in humans. Once you commit yourself to do this, it is not difficult. Anthropometrics has important relevance in ergonomic research and dermatoglyphics is essential in many criminal justice studies.

Goals and Objectives

The goal of this lab is to introduce students to the use of calipers and other measuring devices used in anthropometry and to permit the comparative assessment of various anthropometric parameters. Students will also have the opportunity in this lab to explore dermatoglyphics and anthroposcopy.

Key Terms and Topics

opposition movement, extension movement, flexion movement, anterior, posterior, distal, proximal, midsagittal plane, parasagittal, frontal transverse plane, coronal plane, mesial and distal teeth, lingual, labial, buccal dental orientations, phalanges, tarsus, ulna, radium, humerus, sternum, scapula, pubis, ischium, cranium, vertebrae, femur, patella, tibia, fibula, metatarsals

Pre-Lab Assignments

1. Review the anatomical terms in your glossary. Be familiar with these terms and their locations in the intact primate skeleton.
2. View the following Internet sites prior to the lab and study the excellent material contained therein:
   a. Gray's Anatomy—http://www.bartleby.com/107
   b. The Virtual Body—http://www.medtropolis.com/VBody.asp
   c. The Visible Embryo—http://www.visembryo.com/baby/index.html
   d. Visible Human Cross Sections—http://www.meddean.luc.edu/lumen/MedEd/GrossAnatomy/cross-section/index.html
   e. Primates—http://sss.primates.com
   f. Primates Fact Sheet—http://members.tripod.com/cacajao/factsheets.html

Laboratory Activities

Laboratory Activity 1. Identification and matching of radiographic and actual skeletal samples

View the radiographs provided in this laboratory and use the skeletal charts and models in the laboratory to identify which parts of the body are depicted. Compare these same structures in the various nonhuman primate skeletons available in the laboratory. Note the ways in which these parts are similar and dissimilar among various species and between genders of the same species. Look at the materials presented at each station. Keep detailed notes of your observations and make drawings of key anatomical components. Commit these to memory. Be prepared to discuss your findings during this laboratory.

Laboratory Activity 2. Comparing various anthropometric and anthroposcopic measurements from modern humans

Anthropometry is the system of measurements and observations of humans. This can include measurements of the body, documentation of various blood types, testing for different abilities and senses, and observations of morphological differences. Usually an anthropologist has a specific trait in mind before starting to take measurements or make observations, and this trait has some relevance to his or her research. In this lab you will perform a variety of tasks to collect data on yourself and your classmates, and you will analyze the data and present it in a meaningful scientific format. Again, since you will be making scientific measurements, you must use the metric system. All of the tools you will use are calibrated in centimeters (cm) and millimeters (mm). An inch is equal to 2.54 cm. Working in pairs, take the following measurements and record them in the table of class anthropometric and anthroposcopic measurements. **Be sure to take all of your measurements on the right side for consistency.**

Classical Anthropometric Traits Background Information

Anthropometry is an essential component of the study of growth, development, and variation. Traits of complex inheritance include body size, body form, cormic index (sitting height divided by standing height), inemenbral index (ratio of arm to leg length), steatopygia (concentration of enlarged fat cells supported by bands of fibrous tissue in the gluteal region), body weight, head size and shape (cephalic index), and nasal index. Many of these polygenic traits are correlated with protracted, multigenerational residence in particular geographical regions. Indeed, variation in polygenic traits provides some of the strongest evidence available for the interaction of genes and environment. Biological anthropology has historically had strong roots in anatomy and hence there has been a long interest in the measurement and significance of variation in these complex aspects of human biodiversity.

Anthropometer

Stature—Subject is shoeless, with back against the wall and head oriented in the Frankfort plan. Measure from the floor to the vertex of the head, taking care that the instrument is vertical. (cm)

Sitting height—Subject is seated, so that feet are off the floor, and preferably the back is against a wall or other vertical surface. Measure from the seated surface to the vertex of the head. (cm)

Head height—From porion (upper margin of the external auditory meatus, or ear hole) to the vertex of the head. Head is in the Frankfort plane. (mm)

Tape

Span—Subject has arms stretched horizontally against the wall. Measure the distance from the tip of one middle finger to the tip of the other. (cm)

Head circumference—Measure from glabella to opisthocranion, keeping the instrument in the midline of the head. (mm)

Spreading Caliper

Head length—Measure from glabella to opisthocranion, keeping the instrument in the midline of the head. (mm)

Head breadth—This is the maximum breadth of the head wherever found (above and behind the ears) in a plane perpendicular to the midline. (mm)

Record the presence or absence of the following traits:

Tongue rolling—The ability to roll the edges of the tongue upward. (dominant trait)

Earlobe attachment—The lower part of the earlobe is either attached to the skin of the head or free. Some people have partially attached lobes; score these as attached. (Attachment is a recessive trait.)

Darwin's tubercle—This is a projection or thickening of the cartilage on the most superior-posterior edge of the ear. (dominant trait)

Fill out a handedness form and record the handedness quotient for each individual in the table.

Compute and record cranial capacity using the following formulae:

For females:

$$[(0.0004) \times (\text{head length}-11) \times (\text{head breadth}-11) \times (\text{head height}-11)] + 206.6$$

For males:

$$[(0.000337) \times (\text{head length}-11) \times (\text{head breadth}-11) \times (\text{head height}-11)] + 406.01$$

Obtain data from the rest of the class so that you have information on a population of at least 18 individuals.

Instructions for Anthropometric/Anthroposcopic Table

Using the equipment and supplies provided, measure the parameters indicated for yourself and your classmates. Then calculate the mean lab group values (plus or minus their standard deviations). Graph these and compare your individual values with the averages for your lab.

TABLE OF CLASS MEASUREMENTS

	1 Self	2	3	4	5	6	7	8	9	10	11	12	13	14	15	16	17	18
Age	18																	
Sex	F																	
Height (self report)	1005.6 mm																	
Height (MVA)	—																	
Stature	1590																	
Sitting Height	880																	
Head Height	131																	
Span	1556																	
Head Circumference	533																	
Head Length	190																	
Head Breadth	145																	
Tongue Roll (P/A)	P																	
Earlobe Attachment (P/A)	A																	
Darwin's Tubercle (P/A)	P																	
Handedness Quotient	24																	
Limb Dominance	R																	
Cranial Capacity																		

Span - finger tip to finger tip?
head length - forhead to back of head
head breath - above ear on both sides

everything mm
inch → cm → mm
x2.54   x10

59

Comparative Primate Anatomy   65

Assessment of Handedness

QUESTION: Have you ever had any tendency to left-handedness? __yes__

QUESTION: Which foot do you prefer to kick with? __both__

QUESTION: Which eye do you use when using only one? __left__

QUESTION: When you cross your hands, which is on top? __left__

For the following 20 items, indicate your preference in the use of hands in these activities by putting a plus (+) in the appropriate column. Where the preference is so strong that you would never try to use the other hand unless absolutely forced, put two plus signs (++). If in any case you are really indifferent, put a + in both columns. Some of the activities require both hands. In these cases, the part of the task (or object) related to hand preference is indicated in parentheses.

		L	R
1	Writing		++
2	Drawing	+	+
3	Throwing		+
4	Scissors		++
5	Comb	+	+
6	Toothbrush	+	+
7	Knife (without fork)	+	+
8	Spoon		+
9	Hammer		+
10	Screwdriver	+	+
11	Tennis racket	+	+
12	Knife (with fork)	+	+
13	Baseball bat	+	+
14	Golf club (lower hand)	+	+
15	Broom (upper hand)	+	+
16	Rake (upper hand)	+	+
17	Striking match (match)	+	+
18	Opening box (lid)	+	+
19	Dealing cards (card being dealt)		++
20	Threading needle (needle or thread, according to which is moved)	+	+
	TOTAL NUMBER OF +		

Add up the total number of + signs in each column of the box.

$$\text{Handedness Quotient} = \frac{(\text{Total} + \text{in R column}) - (\text{Total} + \text{in L column})}{(\text{Total} + \text{in R column}) + (\text{Total} + \text{in L column})} \times 100$$

The range of handedness is −100 (entirely left-handed) to +100 (entirely right-handed)

$$\frac{23 - 14}{23 + 14} = \frac{9}{37} \times 100 = 24\%$$

Handedness as Determined by Relative Limb Dominance

Give yourself a plus (+) for any right-handed response and a minus (–) for a left-handed response.

QUESTION: Which arm is on top when you fold your arms? ___+___

QUESTION: Which hand is on top when you clap your hands? ___+___

QUESTION: Which thumb is on top when you fold your hands? ___–___

Determine your classification from the following table.

Pattern   a _+_   b _+_   c _–_   Degree_II_

Pattern	Handedness Groups Commonly Represented	Degree
a+b+c+	Extreme right-handed; ambi-handed	I
a+b+c–	Maximum ambi-handed; right-handed	II
a–b+c+	Right-handed	III
a–b+c–	Right-handed; ambi-handed	IV
a+b–c+	Weak left-handed; weak ambi-handed	V
a+b–c–	Left-handed; ambi-handed	VI
a–b–c+	Left-handed	VII
a–b–c–	Extreme left-handed	VIII

How do these measures compare to your previous ideas about handedness?

What is the relationship between handedness and limb preference?

Laboratory Activity 3. Brain weight and body weight

Among marsupials and most placental mammals, there is generally a uniform relationship between brain weight and body weight. However, primates deviate from this pattern somewhat. In the graph presented below, the average values for brain and body weights are plotted. The diagonal regression line represents the line of best fit to the plotted points. Study this graph and answer the following questions:

a. Why is brain weight plotted against body weight in comparisons of encephalization (relative brain size) instead of making direct comparisons of brain size?

b. What does the position of primates (P) mean and what are the evolutionary consequences of this?

c. If you were to graph the brain and body weights of hominoids (including various fossil hominids), what sort of results would you expect? (You can draw a hypothetical graph to illustrate this.)

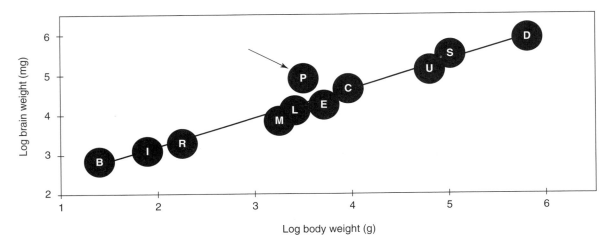

KEY
B = bats
C = carnivores
D = whales and dolphins
E = edentates (sloth, New World anteaters and armadillos)
I = insectivores and tree shrews
L = lagomorphs (rabbits and hares)
M = marsupials
P = primates
R = rodents
S = seals and sea lions
U = hoofed mammals (ungulates)

Laboratory Activity 4. Comparative dermatoglyphics

While you are considering your hands, look at the dermal ridge configurations on the digits and palms. These dermal ridges begin to develop about the thirteenth week of prenatal life and the pattern is complete by the nineteenth week. What are your own dermal patterns?

The patterns on the fingertips are of the three basic types, the arches, loops, and whorls or mixtures of them. The loops may be ulnar or radial loops. The pattern frequencies vary somewhat by sex with females having slightly more arches and fewer whorls than males. Geographical differences also exist with East Asians having a higher frequency of whorls than Europeans. A triradius is a three-way fork, a confluence of three ridge systems. Arches have no triradii, a loop has one, and the whorl has two or more. A triradius is seen at the base of the palm, the axial triradius.

Did You Know?

The dermatoglyphic features commonly seen in the hands of those with various chromosomal abnormalities differ from the dermatoglyphic patterns seen normally. Trisomy 21 includes an increased incidence of ulna loops (83%) (normally 63%) which are very high and L shaped. They have a reduced incidence of whorls (12%) and arches (3%) and a prominent Simian Crease (50%). The crease is a single distal transverse crease across the palms.

Individuals with the 47, XXY karyotype tend to have an excess of arches, while individuals with Turner syndrome (X0) tend to have a predominance of whorls. Individuals with Trisomy 13 karyotype tend to have an excess of arches and 60% have the Simian Crease. Individuals affected with Cri du Chat (crying cat) syndrome (5p-) have an excess of arches and 90% have the Simian Crease.

Dermatoglyphics is increasingly used to diagnose important congenital defects.

3. Cranial Capacity [1,357.93]

Post-Lab Assignments

(due at the beginning of the next laboratory)

these 3 things

1. For each variable measured or observation made, calculate the mean and standard deviation for the group. Graph your results and indicate where your personal values lie relative to the group norms.

2. Develop several testable hypotheses based upon your research results. How would you test these hypotheses further?

LAB 5

Primate Taxonomy and Systematics

OBJECTIVES

- Taxonomic classification and systematics simulation activity
- Cladistic interpretations of primate molecular genetic variations
- Contrasting models of contemporary primate taxonomy

There are over 190 species of living primates and each has distinctive traits. By studying the shared and evolved traits of modern primates, we can gain insight into the early evolutionary forces that may have shaped ancestral primates and produced the current broad variation in contemporary primates. Great diversity exists among the living as well as extinct primates. In this lab, we will continue our study of the differences and similarities among living primates by focusing on the use of molecular genetics in resolving questions of taxonomic affinity. We will also discuss how anatomical, physiological, behavioral, ecological, genetic, and other traits are synthesized in the creation of taxonomies.

Every known living (and extinct) plant and animal has been assigned a home in the scientific taxonomic hierarchy. These assignments designate evolutionary relationships between classified groups, and the placement of the groups into larger classifications is based on what we currently understand of their genetic closeness and evolutionary history. You may be familiar with some of the genus and species names—*Homo sapiens,* for instance, or *Drosophila melanogaster* (fruit fly), if you remember your high school biology. Note that the genus name is capitalized but the species name is not, and the whole name is italicized. These names were assigned only after the organisms were placed into a hierarchy showing where they belong with respect to all other organisms. The hierarchy consists of several levels starting at the top with Kingdom. The structure of this classification, using one classification for humans as an example is:

KINGDOM   Animalia
    PHYLUM   Chordata
       CLASS   Mammalia
         ORDER   Primates
           FAMILY   Hominidae
             GENUS   Homo
               SPECIES   sapiens
                 SUBSPECIES   sapiens

Other categories may also be included such as "Superfamilies" or "Infraorder," etc. It is usually easy to decide where a multi-celled organism fits at the Kingdom level (Kingdom separation is still debated for single-celled organisms). However, as organisms are ranked in the lower parts of the hierarchy, it gets more difficult to categorize them.

Purpose of This Laboratory

Taxonomy is a vital part of many areas of biological anthropology. By systematically and scientifically classifying the world around us, we are able to make order out of often overwhelming biological variation. Accurate taxonomic classification gives us an evolutionary perspective on the life forms we are ordering as well. This laboratory gives you insight on the basic principles of taxonomy and their application to the order Primates.

Goals and Objectives

The goal of this lab is to show how the science of taxonomy (classification) works and what problems and challenges are associated with assigning an animal to a particular slot in the classification. This lab also exposes students to the anatomical diversity among living primates.

Key Terms and Topics

prosimians, strepsirhini, haplorhini, rhinarium, prehensile tail, Y-5 molar pattern, brachiation, bipedalism, diastema, anthropoids, hominoid, catarrhine, platyrrhine, heterondontism, sexual dimorphism, era, period, epoch, mya

Pre-Lab Assignments

(due at the beginning of the lab)

1. Identify the two major subdivisions of the order Primates.

2. Identify which major groups of primates are included among the anthropoidea.

3. Review and learn the names of the bones in the primate skeleton (this should be easy since you were working on this during the last lab as well).

4. What are the differences between an ape and a monkey?

5. What kind of primate was *Gigantopithecus?* (Decode the name)

Laboratory Activities

Laboratory Activity 1. Taxonomy classification and systematics simulation activity

Working together in groups of four or five, examine the bag of fossil "organisms" on your tables. Many of these "organisms" are newly discovered and have not been classified taxonomically. This is your job: to determine the best classification scheme for the diversity of organisms available to you. In order to accomplish this task, you must think as a taxonomist would:

a. Spread the fossils out and look at the diversity of the sample.

b. You are to classify these organisms into six to ten species, and to document your system with characteristics and sort them together.

c. You might decide that you have several genera, related or otherwise. Be consistent and systematic about how you sort the fossils.

d. Describe the species in terms of their unique or important characteristic. Use shape, size, color, texture—anything you think is important.

e. Keep in mind that many species exhibit sexual dimorphism, and some may have different forms throughout life (such as larvae, pupae, and two-winged creatures). Traditionally in taxonomy, the team describing new species, genera, and families has the privilege of naming the new species. However, future scientists must be able to decipher your system.

When taxonomy is applied to groups derived from different time periods, you can see an evolutionary schematic representing the history of the organisms. Some organisms retain distinct characteristics from their ancestors, and some are more difficult to assign.

a. Decide which of your species are closely related and which are not related, based on characteristics you used to describe species.

b. Diagram the relationship of the species, using categories genus, family, and order.

QUESTION: What kinds of additional information about the "organisms" would you want to obtain to assist in the (accurate) classification?

QUESTION: Did you use cladistics or traditional systematics when you classified the "organisms"?

QUESTION: Speculate on what features the ancestors of your genera and families might have exhibited, and what adaptive niches they might have filled.

Participate in an in-lab discussion of the various classification schemes that the different groups of students come up with and their rationalizations for these schemes.

Laboratory Activity 2. Cladistic analysis based on comparison of mtDNA sequences of humans, chimpanzees, gorillas, and orangutans

Determine the evolutionary relationship among the species based on the partial mtDNA sequences of the four genera presented below. Here are the steps you should follow:

1. Start by counting the number of base pair differences between each pair of species in the FIRST SIX lines of sequence. Note the similarities and differences. (HINT: It is easier to place the base pairs on a pre-segmented sheet, such as graft paper and then make your comparisons. Graft paper is provided in your Workbook.)

QUESTION: How much do humans, gorillas, and chimpanzees differ in their mtDNA sequences?

QUESTION: Do you see any patterns between species?

QUESTION: Which primates appear most similar to each other?

The sequence data shown is only a portion of the total 16569 base pairs in the mtDNA genome. You should also note that you are looking at only one strand of the double-stranded DNA molecule.

- Record this data and carefully review the results.
- On the basis of the differences and similarities you uncover, build your own draft cladogram of the likely evolutionary relationships among these species. (Your TA will help you with this effort.)
- Compare the five cladistic diagrams in this lab to your cladogram.
- Identify which of the five cladograms agrees best with your results.
- Discuss your results in lab.

Comparative Hypothetical Primate Molecular Genetic Sequences Exercise

Homo sapiens HUMAN BEING	vs.	*Pan troglodytes* CHIMPANZEE	vs.	*Gorilla gorilla* GORILLA	vs.	*Pongo pygmaeus* ORANGUTAN

mtDNA Line #1

Homo sapiens gatcacaggt	ctatcaccct	attaaccact	cacgggagct	ctccatgcat		ttggtatttt
Pan troglodytes gtatacttca	aaggatactt	aacttaaacc	ccctacgtat	ttatatagag		gagataagtc
Gorilla gorilla caaaggacat	ttaactaaaa	cccctacgca	tctatataga	ggagataagt		cgtaacatgg
Pongo pygmaeus cgcatctata	tagaggaggc	aagtcgtaac	atggtaagcg	tactggaaag		actgcacca

mtDNA Line #2

Homo sapiens cgtctggggg	gtatgcacgc	gatagcattg	cgagacgctg	gagccggagc		accctatgtc
Pan troglodytes gtaacatggt	aagtgtactg	gaaagtgcac	ttggacgaac	cagagtgtag		cttaacataa
Gorilla gorilla taagtgtact	ggaaagtgca	cttggacgaa	ccagagtgta	gcttaacaca		aagcacccaa
Pongo pygmaeus cgaaccagag	ggtagcttaa	cacaaagcac	ccggcttaca	cctgggagat		ttcaattcaa

mtDNA Line #3

Homo sapiens gcagtatctg	tctttgattc	ctgcctcatc	ctattattta	tcgcacctac		gttcaatatt
Pan troglodytes agcacccaac	ttacacttag	gagatttcaa	ctcaacttga	ccactctgag		ccaaacctag
Gorilla gorilla cttacactta	ggagatttca	actcaacttg	accgctctga	gcaaaaccta		gccccaaacc
Pongo pygmaeus cctggcccct	ctgagctaac	ttacttgg	aacccaaccc	accttactac		caaccaaccc

mtDNA Line #4

Homo sapiens acaggcgaac	atacttacta	aagtgtgtta	attaattaat	gcttgtagga		cataataata
Pan troglodytes ccccaaaccc	cctccaccct	actaccaaac	aaccttaacc	aaaccattta		cccaaataaa
Gorilla gorilla caccccacat	tactaccaaa	caactttaat	caaaccattt	acccaaataa		agtataggcg
Pongo pygmaeus taaccaaacc	tactaccaaa	caacgtata	ggcgatagaa	attacaatcc		ggcgcaatag

mtDNA Line #5
Homo sapiens
| acaattgaat | gtctgcacag | ccActtttcca | cacagacatc | ataacaaaaa | atttccacca |

Pan troglodytes
| gtataggcga | tagaaattgt | aaaccggcgc | aatagacata | gtaccgcaag | ggaaagatga |

Gorilla gorilla
| atagaaattg | taaatcggcg | caatagatat | agtaccgcaa | gggaaagatg | aaaaaatata |

Pongo pygmaeus
| acacagtacc | gtaagggaaa | gatgaaaaaa | cacaaccaag | cacaacatag | caaggactaa |

mtDNA Line #6
Homo sapiens
| aacccccct | CCCCCgcttc | tggccacagc | acttaaacac | atctctgcca | aaccccaaaa |

Pan troglodytes
| aaaattatac | ccaagcataa | tacagcaagg | actaacccct | gtaccttttg | cataatgaat |

Gorilla gorilla
| accaagcatg | acacagcaag | gactaacccc | tgtaccttct | gcataatgaa | ttaactagaa |

Pongo pygmaeus
| cccctgtacc | ttttgcataa | tgaattaact | agaaacaacc | ttgcaaggag | agccaaagcc |

Cladistic Relationships of Modern Apes and Modern Humans as Revealed by Molecular Genetic mtDNA Data

QUESTION: Which option best fits your comparative data on the first six lines of mtDNA code?

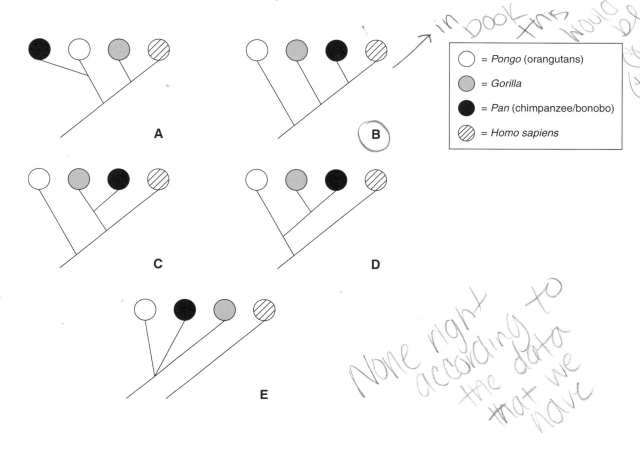

= Pongo (orangutans)

= Gorilla

= Pan (chimpanzee/bonobo)

= Homo sapiens

[handwritten: in book this would be the correct (the DNA is a little different)]

[handwritten: None right according to the data that we have]

Laboratory Activity 3. Contrasting taxonomic models for contemporary primates

Taxonomies attempt to group species into broader categories (taxa, sing. taxon) on the basis of substantial similarities and inferred descent from common ancestors. The primate order is divisible into numerous biological taxa on several levels. There are several possible taxonomical systems, and these have changed over time. Your text emphasizes the sterpsirhini-haplorhini classification system. Please learn this system and be able to associate representative primates with each level.

Look carefully at the primate skeletons on display in the lab. Now, follow this sequence of activities to better understand the relationship between taxonomy and anatomy.

a. First review the names of the bones listed in Appendix 1 of your text.

b. Then carefully study the primate skeletons on display, noting the name of the primate and its location in the taxonomic scheme presented in your Lab Notebook.

c. Make comparative assessments of these skeletons.

d. Identify at least 10 anatomical similarities and differences among the various primates on display.

e. Identify which specimens are probably most closely related and give reasons for your decision.

f. For each similarity or difference, briefly discuss the adaptive significance of the feature.

QUESTION: Can you identify any shared, derived features within this group of primate skeletons?

g. Look again at the primate classification scheme.

QUESTION: Which suborders are represented among the primate skeletons?

h. Compare the following simplified primate taxonomy with more extensive taxonomies. Other than in detail, in what ways are they similar and in which ways do they differ?

Simplified Primate Taxonomy

Order	Suborder	Infraorder	Super Family	Family	Common Term
Primates					
	Prosimii				Loris
					Lemur
					Tarsier
		Platyrrhini		Callitrichidae and Cebidae	New World Monkeys
	Anthropoidea				
		Catarrhini	Cercopithecoidea	Colobinae and Cercopithecinae	Old World Monkeys
	Hominoidea			Hylobatidae	Gibbons
					Simangs
				Pongidae	Orangutans
					Gorillas
					Chimpanzees
					Bonobos
				Hominidae	Humans

Additional Background Information

When two or more organisms have similar structures (e.g., human arms and bird wings) with a similar genetic basis, we speak of these as homologous structures. In general, the more homologies two groups of organisms share, the closer their genetic relationship and the more recently they have shared a common ancestor. When homologous organisms are evaluated in an evolutionary time framework, scientists are able to construct phylogenetic trees. When the structures of various organisms are functionally similar but have a very different hereditary basis, they are considered analogous structures (e.g., bat wings and mosquito wings). Taxonomy owes its modern origins in western science to Linnaeus who initiated the bionomial system using two terms: the genus and the species (e.g., *Homo sapiens*). In modern usage, these two descriptive terms, the genus and the species, are always either in italics or underlined. The first letter of the genus name is capitalized while the species name remains entirely in lowercase letters. To this we add a subspecies designation that is also lowercase and italicized (or underlined) (e.g., *Homo sapiens sapiens*). The subspecies designation is the biological race name. Review the generalized Linnaean hierarchy of zoological classification. Each level represents a more exclusive level than the previous level to the left.

The living primates can be grouped according to grades. While **grade one** is not really a primate at all but is an insectivorous (insect-eating) rodent-like creature, **grade two** (lorises and lemurs) are clearly primates although they have retained many of the primitive ancestral traits of the earliest primates. Most lemurs live on the island of Madagascar (off the coast of East Africa) where they have had the freedom to diversify and expand into a number of niches without competition from monkeys or apes. This adaptive radiation continued until humans came to the island relatively recently. Lorises have a broad distribution in Africa and Asia but most have had to adopt a nocturnal (night-time) activity pattern. This is reflected in the large size of their eyes.

The tarsiers represent the **third grade** of primates. Originally they were classified with the lemurs and lorises (because they superficially resemble these animals anatomically). However, recent molecular studies of the tarsiers and more sophisticated anatomical assessments suggest to some researchers that these animals are more akin to modern monkeys than they are to the lemurs and lorises.

Grade four of the primates consists of monkeys. Basically, there are the New World monkeys and the Old World monkeys. The former are almost always arboreal, have a nose shape that is broad with wildly flaring nostrils that face outwards (platyrrhine), and have one or more premolar teeth than do the Old World monkeys. Old World monkeys have nostrils that face downward (catarrhine) and have dental patterns that are more similar to the apes.

The **fifth grade** of primates is represented by the hominoids. These include the gibbon and siamang, the orangutan, the gorilla, the chimpanzee, and the bonobo. Human beings are included in this grade as well.

QUESTION: Can you think of a reason why humans are classified among the apes?

Some of the shared anatomical features of the human, chimpanzee, and gorilla craniofacial skeleton are:

1. The nasal aperture is broad.
2. The subnasal plane is truncated and stepped down to the floor of the nasal cavity.
3. The orbits are approximately square and often broader than they are high.
4. The interorbital distance is large.
5. The intraorbital foramina are usually three to less in number and are situated on or close to the zygomaticomaxillary suture.
6. The zygomatic bone is usually curved and has a pronounced posterior slope.
7. The one or two zygomatic foramina (holes in the zygomatic bone for transmission of nerves and blood vessels to the side of the face) are small and are situated at or below the lower rim of the orbits.
8. The glabella is thickened.
9. The palate has small incisive fossae and large, oval-shaped greater palatine foramina (small holes in the posterior part of the hard palate for passage of nerves and blood vessels to the back of the palate).
10. The teeth are basically similar in cusp pattern.

Make sure that you understand what each of these 10 stated facts means anatomically!

Post-Lab Assignment

(due at the beginning of the next lab)

From your TA, select a card that lists five primates at random. For each primate listed, give their scientific name and common name, locate them taxonomically (identify their suborder, infraorder, subfamily, and family), and describe their natural habitat. Note also any unusual anatomical, physiological, or behavioral features of each. If you can find a picture of each primate, include these in your report. Make your report on your five unique primates three to four pages 12-font typed, double-spaced pages in length. This report is due at the beginning of the next lab.

LAB 6

Primate Social Behavior

OBJECTIVES

- Documented observations of primate social behaviors
- Primate Jeopardy game
- Behavioral data interpretation and extrapolation

The accurate and systematic observation and analysis of primate behavior is essential for successful conservation efforts and for a more complete understanding of ourselves as human beings. Many species of primates are facing extinction as their habitats are shrinking. Only by careful research of these complex animals can we help to save them, facilitate their reproduction, and preserve their genetic heterogeneity. The observation and evaluation of primate social behavior enriches our perspective on the evolution of human behavior patterns. This is especially useful since bone and artifact remains of extinct hominids give anthropologists only a limited view of the primate ethogram, or behavior repertoire.

Early nonhuman primate observations made by anthropologists have focused on the savanna dwellers like the baboons (*Papio* spp) and the African forest-dwelling apes, such as the chimpanzee and bonobos (*Pan* spp) and the gorilla (*Gorilla*). Baboons have been studied largely because it was believed that they occupied the same ecological niche as some of the early hominids. More recent evidence suggests that the first hominids were actually living in forested environments. Chimpanzees, bonobos, and gorillas are studied because of their close genetic similarities to modern humans (*Homo sapiens sapiens*).

Purpose of This Laboratory

Behavior is an important component of taxonomy and systematics. Behavior can also give evolutionary insight into the origins of certain behavioral responses in related species. Biological anthropologists depend upon careful assessments of primate behavior to understand the species in question and its relationship to its environment. Armed with this information, these scientists can extrapolate to other past and present species.

Goals and Objectives

The goals of this laboratory are to increase the student's knowledge of the range of primate social behaviors, to learn to identify specific behaviors, and to evaluate the correspondence between these behaviors (in non-human primates) and similar behaviors in humans.

Key Terms and Topics

reproductive efficiency, effectance motivation, behavioral affinities, cooperative hunting, pair-bonding, core area, dominance, territoriality, core area, adaptive niche, grooming, hierarchy, kin selection, single-male group, multi-male group

Pre-Lab Assignment

Observe people around campus, at work, at home, and during holidays and vacations. Pay close attention to nonverbal communication such as hand gestures, leg position when sitting, movement of the eyes, inclination of the body, etc. Notice how people exert their authority or reinforce their submissiveness with body language. Observe people in different social situations and observe people from different cultural and economic backgrounds. What differences and similarities do you see? Log two pages of notes on what behaviors are used in each setting. Turn in this log at the beginning of this lab.

Laboratory Activities

Laboratory Activity 1. Observations of nonhuman primate behaviors

Use the score sheets provided for your assessments of nonhuman primate behaviors. During this lab, you will observe several video clips of behaviors for different primate species. For each species, record the MAJOR behavior that is taking place. Use a timer to keep track of the time frame of your observations. When you are doing this activity, there will be little time for discussion during the observations, so make sure you look over the behaviors checklist before you start viewing the primate behavioral videos. Work with a partner in scoring the behaviors. Enter your data into the class database and use the group data for hypothesis development and testing.

Follow these steps:

1. Review the Primate Behavior Score Sheet categories.
2. View the video clips, paying careful attention to the actual activities of the primate participants.
3. Document your observations of the primate behavior at timed intervals.
4. Looking at only your own data, develop two testable hypotheses concerning primate behavior.
5. Enter your observational data into the class database.
6. Download the class database when completed and use this group data to test your two hypotheses.
7. Contrast your null and alternative hypotheses with the results generated from the group data.
8. Perform a simple statistical assessment of the group data, using an alpha level of 0.05 to determine statistical significance.
9. For HOMEWORK, type a one- to two-page summary of your results and the interpretation of their meaning.

NOTE: Four Primate Behavior Score Sheets are provided. Make at least two complete observations and develop your hypotheses from these.

Primate Behavior Score Sheet

Species: _____ **Sex** _____ **Age** _____

Location: _____

Time 15 sec Interval	Posture-Locomotion	Ground (G) OR Above Ground (AG)	Other Behavior (see codes)
0–15			
30			
45			
1:00			
1:15			
1:30			
1:45			
2:00			
2:15			
2:30			
2:45			
3:00			
3:15			
3:30			
3:45			
4:00			
4:15			
4:30			
4:45			
5:00			
5:15			
5:30			
5:45			
6:00			

Posture and Locomotion
P = prone
S = sit
ST = stand
W = walking
SW = swinging
H = hanging

Other Behaviors
GO = grooming other
GR = being groomed
GA = autogroom
S = scratch
F = feed

R = resting
M = moving
L = looking
A = affiliative other than grooming
AG = aggressive/fighting

Other comments:

Laboratory Activity 2. Primate Jeopardy game

In the second part of this laboratory, students will compete in teams to play "Primate Jeopardy." Following the general rules for the television show "Jeopardy," each team will be permitted to select a category and will identify the most appropriate question for the answer provided. In the course of competing, students will have an opportunity to demonstrate their knowledge of various aspects of primate social behavior. Categories for consideration will include details of social groupings, dietary patterns, ecological range, mating patterns, taxonomic identifications, and other aspects of primate behavior.

Primate Jeopardy Answer Categories

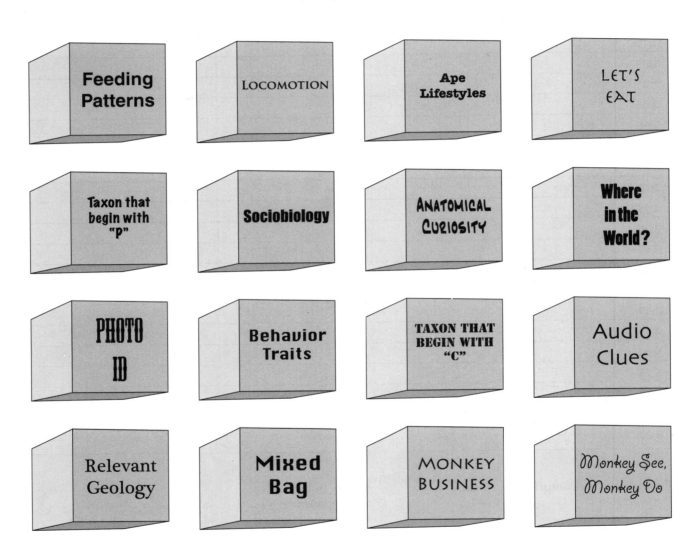

Laboratory Activity 3. Interpretation and discussion of primate behavior

Review the bar graph presented below and participate in a class discussion of its interpretation, answering the questions posed and generating additional questions on your own.

PRIMATE BEHAVIOR
Male Dominance and Reproductive Success

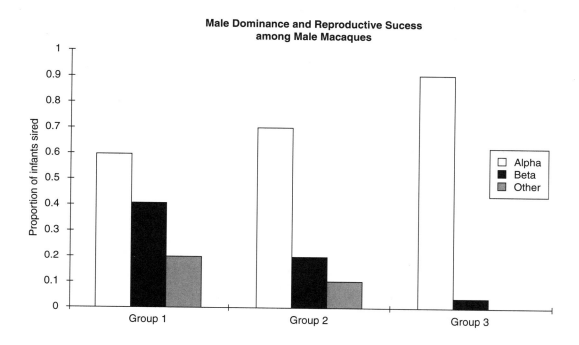

In three groups of free-ranging (noncaptive) long-tailed macaques, the highest-ranking (alpha) male fathered a much larger fraction of infants than the second-ranking (beta) male and other low-ranking males did.

QUESTION: What are the behavioral implications of this pattern on each group?

QUESTION: What are the genetic consequences for subsequent generations of macaques when male dominance is positively correlated with reproductive success?

QUESTION: What is the applicability, if any, of these findings to modern humans?

Post-Lab Assignment

(due next lab period)

Construct four graphs comparing behaviors among the various primate groups and write one to two paragraphs discussing the results illustrated in each graph. Two of the graphs should compare behavioral differences between species. The third graph should contrast behaviors between male and female members of the same species. The fourth graph should contrast behaviors by age in a single species. Remember that humans are primates also!

GRAPH 1: BEHAVIORAL COMPARISONS

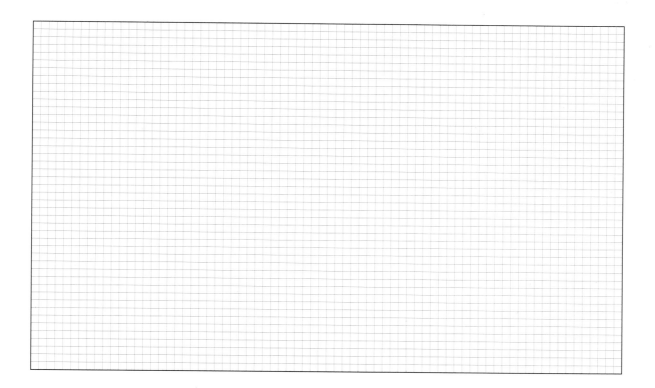

GRAPH 2: BEHAVIORAL COMPARISONS

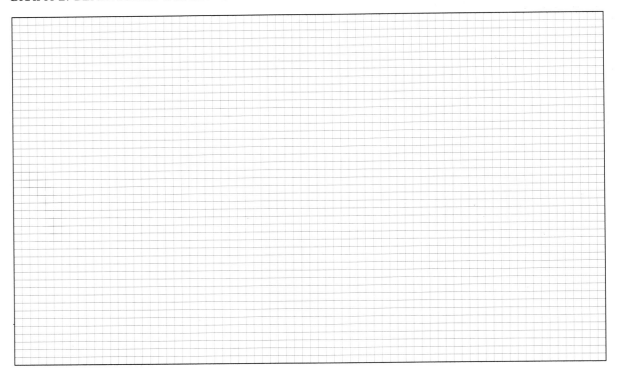

GRAPH 3: BEHAVIORAL COMPARISONS

GRAPH 4: BEHAVIORAL COMPARISONS

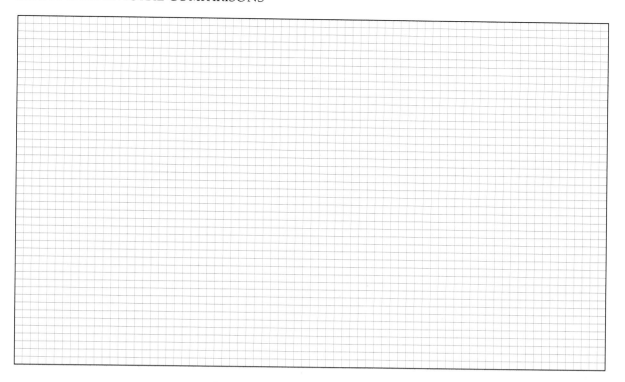

LAB

7

Hominid Anatomical and Behavioral Adaptations 1

OBJECTIVES

- Hominid bipedality: hypothesis testing
- Functional anatomy of handedness and prehensility
- Climate and limb length in archaic and modern humans

Habitual bipedalism is an anatomical and behavioral landmark of hominids. This unique form of locomotion clearly separates the hominid lineage from those of other primates. Pale-oanthropologists have long struggled to explain the ecological and anatomical origins of bipedalism. For a long time, climatic changes were identified as being paramount in the evolution of bipedalism. Scientists thought that the drying of the forested regions and the increased distance between patches of trees caused early proto-hominids to descend from the trees more frequently and spend more time on the ground. As the savanna expanded, proto-hominids who could spend extended periods in a semi-erect posture had a survival advantage (for example, being able to see above the tall grass, detect predators, and identify scavenge sites more efficiently) compared to those proto-hominids who could not. However, recent ecological evidence suggests that the climatic factors were not as relevant as originally believed. Now alternative models to the "savanna hypothesis" are being proposed.

Purpose of This Laboratory

Biological anthropologists have long studied primate locomotion. This allows us to develop hypotheses about the specifics of human evolution. In this lab, students will test various hypotheses concerning bipedality and other forms of locomotion observed among the primates, they will evaluate hand preference, and investigate the utility of prehensility. Finally, the lab will discuss and develop hypotheses concerning the ecological constraints associated with differences in limb length in archaic and modern humans.

Goals and Objectives

In this laboratory, students will work individually and in teams to explore many dimensions of habitual bipedalism, as expressed throughout the life span. Students will also simulate semi-bipedalism, quadrupedalism, knuckle-walking, and other modes of locomotion in an effort to understand the advantages and limitations of each. Primate prehensility will be reenacted and various hypotheses concerning efficacy tested. As a third objective, students will become familiar with the early geographical range of hominids and identify the possible selective effects of each environment on various hominid species.

Key Terms and Topics

the adaptationist paradigm, prehensility, binocular vision, stereoscopic vision, bipedalism vs. quadrupedalism, dexterous feet, grasping hands

Pre-Lab Assignment

Observe walking and running characteristics of humans. How are these characteristics influenced by age? By gender? By athletic status? By ethnicity? By body size and shape? Document your observations and report on your insights at the beginning of the lab.

Laboratory Activities

Working in groups of three or four students, each group will conduct the following experiments:

Laboratory Activity 1. Observe the normal human pattern of bipedality and identify the six stages of bipedality

For this activity, groups will use the treadmill and the bare floor. Students should be prepared to walk barefoot and/or in very thin socks/stockings.

Hominid Bipedalism

Carefully observe the human pattern of bipedality. What happens first, second, third, etc.? Identify the six stages of bipedality and give a visual depiction of each stage.

1	2	3
4	5	6

Bipedalism Evaluation Forms

Walking	M/F	Height	Weight	C1	C2	C3	C4
1							
2							
3							
4							
5							
6							
Running/Jogging							
1							
2							
3							
4							
5							
6							

Additional comments on bipedalism experiments: _____

_____

_____

_____

_____

Laboratory Activity 2. Compare the skeletons of several quadrupeds and a biped

Describe differences you observe in the following areas: skull, vertebral column, shoulder girdle, pelvic girdle, lower limbs, ankle, and foot. Observe the isolated elements from several "mystery" specimens and determine whether they belong to a quadruped or a biped. Give reasons for your answers.

Laboratory Activity 3. Create footprints by walking through the sandbox

Take various measurements and observations of differences in stride characteristics that correspond to sex, height/weight, and gait. Record your observations in the walking/running/jogging part of the worksheet and use these for your evaluations below.

Laboratory Activity 4. Practice bipedality under various sets of constraints (as indicated by your instructor)

Record your experiences under each condition. How does the center of gravity change under each set of constraints? What role do the gluteal muscles play in facilitating bipedality under each set of constraints? Keep detailed notes on your observations and be prepared to produce a data table summarizing your results.

Laboratory Activity 5. Practice prehensility (using your hands and feet) under various sets of constraints

Identify the relationship between bipedality and prehensility.

Comparative Prehensility Activity

Many primates have opposable thumbs, but none have a power grip like the human hand. Humans also have excellent fine motor skills, such as are used to hold a pencil, thread a needle, or pick up a dime. But many nonhuman primates have very little control of their fingers except for the thumb and forefinger, with the rest of the fingers following the motion of this latter digit. For example, spider monkeys have lost functional thumbs to facilitate their speedy brachiation through the forest canopy. The aye-aye has evolved a long, skeletal middle finger for digging out grubs.

With your partner, restrict the movement of the hands in various ways to imitate other primates. Try to pick up various objects around the room, open door knobs, unbutton your shirt, and hold a stone. Take notes on your observations of yourself and others.

Attempt prehensility with your feet. What difficulties do you encounter? What could account for these? Some examples of ways to emulate the prehensility of other primates:

1. Tie your thumb to your hand to approximate the prehensility of a spider monkey.
2. Tie your fingers together, leaving the thumb free to approximate an average macaque.
3. Tape an 8-inch stick to your middle finger, and see what you can do. Several test areas are set up for you to evaluate. Keep a record of your observations.
4. Try other variations and record the functional effects. Your TAs will help you with these activities.

The advent of habitual bipedalism among the primates signaled the end of dexterous feet. It has been suggested that the evolutionary trajectory is toward a continued shortening and eventual loss of toes in habitual bipeds. Yet, we still do have toes, and we can use them with some skill to pick up items. Years ago, a child who lacked the use of his arms was able to solve a Rubik's Cube with his feet in less than 2 minutes. While this may be pushing it for most of us, see what you can and cannot pick up with your feet. Record your observations and suggest what specifically is preventing you from being more successful.

Manual Prehensility and Dexterity

Part 1: Have your hands taped as discussed in the laboratory manual. Use the table below to record your assessments of your performance under different conditions of restraint. How is your agility and accuracy affected at each challenge site?

Type of restraint	Retrieving only colored Styrofoam from tanks	Collecting marbles from sand	Removing gummy worm hanging from tree branch (without breaking branch)	Lifting and carrying wooden blocks	Lifting and carrying stones	Squeezing power grip ball (record score)	Unwrapping piece of candy	Picking up seeds and placing in cups	Pinching salt at point A and releasing salt to point B	Picking items from spider's nest	Retrieving snakes and frogs from paper grass in tank
No restraint											
Thumb bound											
4 digits bound											
Elongated middle finger											
Other modification #1											
Other modification #2											

Part 2: Remove your shoes and socks and retrieve pencils using your bare feet. How successful are you? _____

Laboratory Activity 6: Evaluating climate and limb length in archaic and modern humans

People who are indigenous to warm climates tend to have proportionately longer arms and legs relative to the lengths of the trunks than people who are indigenous to cold climates. This increase in length is most pronounced in the distal segment of the limbs. In the graph below, local mean ambient temperature is plotted on the vertical axis. Crural index is plotted on the horizontal axis. The crural index is the ratio of the length of the shin bone (tibia) to the length of the thigh bone (femur). Groups from warm climates tend to have high crural index values. Groups from cold climates tend to have low crural index values. For example, Neanderthals had a crural index similar to the modern day Sami peoples of the Arctic Circle. Review the graph carefully and generate three separate, testable hypotheses based upon the data presented. Be as detailed as possible.

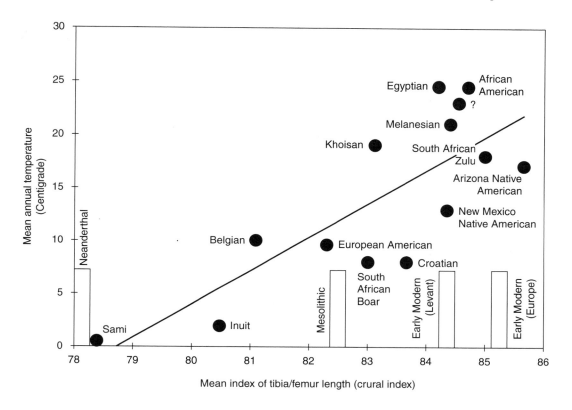

Which population do you think is represented by the ? near the African Americans, Egyptians, and Melanisians? Justify your answer.

LAB 8

Hominid Anatomical and Behavioral Adaptations 2

OBJECTIVES

- Tool development activity
- Tool use and reconstruction of the hominid diet

The first members of our genus, *Homo,* appeared in Africa around 2.5 mya. One of the physical hallmarks of *Homo* is the increase in brain size when compared to earlier hominids. Presumably, larger brains expanded hominid cultural capacity, including the regular manufacture and use of stone tools. While current evidence indicates that some australopithecines used simple Mode I stone tools, the range and sophistication of tool types was greatly expanded by *Homo.*

Modern humans, minus our tools, are far from impressive when compared with other mammals. We are neither exceptionally large, nor strong, nor fast. We cannot easily escape into the trees to avoid predation nor swoop down like a bird of prey to capture other animals. However, humanity has persisted and is now the only extant species of the genus *Homo.* Regular tool manufacture and use has greatly contributed to our cultural and behavioral adaptations to diverse environments while retaining our pronounced genetic similarities.

Many of the most primitive stone tools are almost indistinguishable from ordinary rocks. However, it is the regularity with which they appear and their proximity to other archaeological data that allows for their recognition. Typical tools include the chopper and scraper. Flakes that have been separated from a core tool were also invaluable knife-like tools for early humans.

Purpose of This Laboratory

Understanding how tools are made and used is essential to understanding our species success over the hundreds of thousands of years of our existence. By conceptualizing and using tools, you will be able to experience some of the advantages and limitations of early tool-making technology.

113

Goals and Objectives

The purpose of this lab is to learn about the evolution of the genus *Homo* and to consider some of the cultural developments of the past 2.5 million years. In the lab, students will examine fossil casts and have the opportunity to make and use their own stone and non-stone tools, process raw plant and animal parts, and compare the efficacy of these tools. We will also discuss the evolution of the human diet and the ramifications of evolutionarily recent dietary shifts among modern humans.

Key Terms and Topics

blade, scraper, Oldowan, Acheulean, Mousterian, Neolithic, domestication, human-plant coevolution, human-animal coevolution, agriculture, biotechnology, folivore, frugivore, omnivore, grammivore, dietary requirements, essential nutrients

Pre-Lab Assignment

During which years of hominid evolutionary history were Oldowan, Acheulean, and Mousterian tools made? How can you distinguish among these tools? What tool traditions characterize anatomically and behaviorally modern *Homo sapiens*?

OLDOWAN TOOLS
(Mode 1 tools)

ACHEULEAN TOOLS
(Lower Paleolithic)

MOUSTERIAN TOOLS
(Middle Paleolithic)

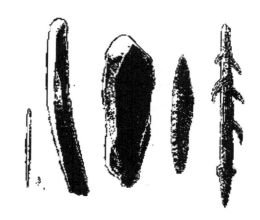

AURIGNACIAN and CHATELPERRONIAN TOOLS
(Upper Paleolithic)

Laboratory Activities

Laboratory Activity 1. Tool conceptualization, manufacture, and use

In this lab, students have an opportunity to make an array of stone and nonstone (e.g., biodegradable) tools from various materials. Students will test the efficiency of their tools in processing common plant and animal materials. In this lab you will make and use your tool(s) to extract marrow from a bone and use a tool to extract "termites" from the mini model termite mounds. Compare your tools against bare hands and against modern tools. Record your observations carefully and supplement your quantitative data with illustrations of the tools you have made. Consider carefully the advantages and limitations of the various tools you have made. What differences do you note in their form?

Important! Before You Begin Making Tools

- You MUST wear protective eye goggles.
- You MUST wear protective gloves if you are working with stone.
- DO NOT hit the desks to make stone tools.
- Please DO NOT use any undesignated surfaces outside.

Please Be Careful!

1. Examine the stone and nonstone tools on display. Compare them with the tools depicted on the previous page.
2. Select stone and nonstone materials for making your own tools.
3. Conceptualize your tool based upon its anticipated use. You may wish to draw a picture of the tool you wish to make, if this will help with your conceptualization process.
4. Begin making your own tools using the techniques relevant in the Pleistocene and early Holocene.
5. Your goal will be to produce tools to be used in several tasks:
   a. Crack a nut
   b. Chop through a small branch
   c. Extract marrow
   d. Cut flesh (not your own!—use the meat provided)
   e. Cut various roots, tubers, and vegetables
   f. Make other tools from the first tool

Take notes on your efforts, draw pictures, and describe the success of each project so you can write up your results for a HOMEWORK report. Use the Tool Assessment Summary Sheets provided. BE SURE TO MAKE AT LEAST THREE DIFFERENT KINDS OF TOOLS AND EVALUATE EACH! YOU CAN TAKE YOUR TOOLS WITH YOU WHEN YOU COMPLETE THIS LAB.

Laboratory Activity 2. Evolution of the human diet

In this part of the lab, we will contrast the typical Western diet consumed in America and a reconstructed Paleolithic diet of our remote ancestors.

1. List the foods and their quantities that you've eaten over the last "typical" 24 hours.

2. List the foods and their quantities that your Paleolithic "alter ego" would have eaten during a "typical" 24-hour period. You will have to do some serious role playing to make these estimations somewhat accurate.

3. Contrast the lists and estimate what minerals, vitamins, fats, proteins, and carbohydrates might distinguish the two diets.

4. Write down your hypotheses regarding the presumed differences in the diet.

5. Evaluate the four Paleolithic diets developed by your instructional staff. How would you rate each (using the criteria presented below as well as other factors you can think of)? What ecosystem would likely support the various diets presented?

Comparative Analysis of Four Reconstructed Paleolithic Meals
(24-hour consumption)

PALEOLITHIC MEAL #1
- CONTENTS
- PALATABILITY
- LIKELY NUTRITIONAL CONTENT
- PRESENTATION
- ECOSYSTEM OF ORIGIN

PALEOLITHIC MEAL #2
- CONTENTS
- PALATABILITY
- LIKELY NUTRITIONAL CONTENT
- PRESENTATION
- ECOSYSTEM OF ORIGIN

PALEOLITHIC MEAL #3
- CONTENTS
- PALATABILITY
- LIKELY NUTRITIONAL CONTENT
- PRESENTATION
- ECOSYSTEM OF ORIGIN

PALEOLITHIC MEAL #4
- CONTENTS
- PALATABILITY
- LIKELY NUTRITIONAL CONTENT
- PRESENTATION
- ECOSYSTEM OF ORIGIN

Overall Comparative Assessments:

_____

_____

_____

_____

_____

_____

_____

_____

_____

_____

_____

_____

_____

_____

_____

_____

_____

_____

_____

_____

_____

_____

_____

_____

_____

Post-Lab Assignments

1. Complete the Tool Assessment Summary Sheets to document your experiences making stone tools. Include descriptions of the materials used, the tools themselves, your success in making them, and how well they worked.

2. Use the USDA website provided by your TA (during the lab) to contrast your "typical" dietary intakes as a modern American and as a Paleolithic hunter-gatherer. Enter both diets into the Internet program, and contrast the analytical results.

3. Prepare a one-page report (single spaced, 11 point font, 1-inch margins, 8 1/2 × 11 inches paper, white, one-sided) on the nutritional and nonnutritional compositional differences between the Paleolithic diet and the modern Western diet. You may use your website dietary contrast and your experiences with our hypothetical Paleolithic diets to help you write your report.

- The quarry stone is used to break the obsidian.
- The obsidian is the black glass that is the tool.
- The billet is used to sharpen.
- The pressure flaker is a smaller stone and pressure is applied with it to break off small flakes.
- Twine is used to attach the tool to a handle.
- The stick is used as the handle to the tool.

- With these materials I made a hammer, knife and scalpel.

- Making the hammer and the knife went really well. The hammer was able to smash things and the knife could slice through a stick. When I was making the scalpel I got an injury on one of my fingers through my protective gloves. The scalpel worked really well and I was able to cut through a piece of paper. Overall this was a good experience making the tools, I did not realize how difficult making these tools really are.

LAB 9

Geological Dating and Paleolithic Reenactments

OBJECTIVES

- Geological dating methods
- Modeling and mapping Middle Stone Age sites
- Construction and analysis of Upper Paleolithic shelters

Bioarchaeology is a critical component of paleoanthropology, the study of ancient (usually fossilized) hominid biological and cultural remains. By carefully studying the past, we are able to develop a better understanding of present patterns of human variation and biocultural diversity. In this laboratory, we will study dating techniques, map a bioarchaeological site, identify significant recovered surface artifacts (with minimal invasion), and at a separate site, reconstruct a life-size model of an Upper Paleolithic shelter for subsequent hypothesis testing.

Purpose of This Laboratory

Paleoanthropology, as an important part of biological anthropology, relies on accurate dating of fossilized remains. In this laboratory you will mimic the work of a field paleoanthropologist as well as gain firsthand knowledge of conceptualizing, building, and residing in a primitive shelter. These experiences will advance your perception on what life was possibly like for our early ancestors, before agriculture, modern technology, and rapid transit.

Goals and Objectives

The goal of this lab is to familiarize students with some of the techniques employed in the dating and interpretation of archaeological materials and to give students the experience of Middle Stone Age shelter conceptualization and construction.

Key Terms and Topics

Upper and Lower Paleolithic Lifeways, artifacts, R1 date, R2 date, R3 date, R4 date, potassium-argon method, half-life, biostratigraphy, chronometric and non-chronomic methods, dendochronology

Pre-Lab Assignments

(due at the beginning of this lab)

1. Review your notes on geological eras and periods. Read the background information on geological dating (below) and be prepared to discuss various dating methods and past geological events.

2. Make a realistic model of a Middle Stone Age shelter and bring it to the lab.

3. Be able to distinguish between relative and absolute dating.

For more depictions and descriptions of shelters from the Paleolithic, please refer to

http://www.personal.psu.edu/users/w/x/wxk116/habitat/
http://www.originsnet.org/eraup.html
http://radar.ngcsu.edu/~jtwynn/paleolithic.htm

Geological Dates and Their Significance

Era	Period	Millions of Years B.P.	Major Evolutionary Events
Azoic		3500–4500	The origin of life
Proterozoic		570–3500	Algae and early invertebrates
Paleozoic	Cambrian	500–570	"Explosion" of life; marine invertebrates
	Ordovician	430–500	Early vertebrates including jawless fishes; trilobites and many other invertebrates
	Silurian	395–430	First fish with jaws; land plants
	Devonian	345–395	Many fish; first amphibians; first forests
	Carboniferous	280–345	Radiation of amphibians; first reptiles and insects
	Permian	230–280	Radiation of reptiles; mammal-like reptiles
Mesozoic	Triassic	180–230	First dinosaurs; egg-laying mammals
	Jurassic	135–180	Dinosaurs dominate; first bird-like reptiles
	Cretaceous	65–135	Extinction of dinosaurs; first birds and placental mammals

Era	Period	Epoch	Millions of Years B.P.	Major Evolutionary Events
Cenozoic	Tertiary	Paleocene	53–65	Primate-like mammals
		Eocene	37–53	First primates (primitive prosimians)
		Oligocene	25–37	Anthropoid radiation (monkeys)
		Miocene	5–25	Radiation of early apes
		Pliocene	1.8–5	First hominids and first members of genus *Homo*
	Quarternary	Pleistocene	0.01–1.8	Evolution of the genus *Homo*
		Holocene	0–0.01	Humans develop agriculture, industry, exploration of outer space

The story of human prehistory has unfolded against a backdrop of massive climatic changes. The Pleistocene, a period of dramatic swing in world climate, is the most recent of the great geological epochs, sometimes called the Age of Humanity. On numerous occasions during the Pleistocene, great ice sheets covered much of western Europe and North America, bringing arctic climate to vast areas of the northern hemisphere. These climatic fluctuations have been documented from deep-sea sediment cores and are evidence of periods of cooler and warmer ocean waters that coincided with major climatic changes ashore.

The Pleistocene began about 1.8 million years ago, during a long-term cooling trend in the world's oceans. This epoch is divided into three periods:

- **The Lower Pleistocene** times lasted until about 700,000 years ago. Analysis of deep-sea cores reveals that the climatic fluctuations between warmer and colder regimens were still relatively minor. These were critical millennia during which humans emerged in Africa and spread from tropical regions into temperate latitudes in Europe and Asia.

- **The Middle Pleistocene** times began with a reversal in the earth's magnetic polarity about 700,000 years ago. The study of paleomagnetism has shown that the earth's geomagnetic field has reversed its polarity many times in the past, reversals that can be studied in volcanic rocks. Since 630,000 years ago there have been at lease eight glacial (cold) and interglacial (warm) cycles, the last cycle ending about 12,000 years ago. These cycles were so constant that it can be said that the world's climate has been in transition from cold to warm, and back again for over 75% of the past 700,000 years. Typically, cold cycles have begun gradually, with vast continental ice sheets forming on land—in Scandinavia, on the Alps, and over the northern parts of North America. These expanded ice sheets locked up enormous quantities of water, causing world sea levels to fall by several hundred feet during glacial episodes. The geography of the world changed dramatically, and large continental shelves were opened up for human settlement. When a warming trend began, deglaciation occurred very rapidly and rising sea levels flooded low-lying coastal areas within a few millennia. During glacial maxima, glaciers covered a full one-third of the earth's land surface.

Throughout the past 700,000 years, vegetational changes have mirrored climatic fluctuations. During glacial episodes, treeless arctic steppe and tundra covered much of Europe and parts of North America, but gave way to temperate forests during interglacials. In the tropics, Africa's Sahara Desert supported grassland during interglacials. During the glacials, however, the desert expanded.

- **The Upper Pleistocene** stage began about 128,000 years ago, with the beginning of the last interglacial. This period lasted until about 118,000 years ago, when a slow cooling trend brought full glacial conditions to Europe and North America. The Würm glaciation (named after a river in the Alps) lasted until about 10,000 years ago, when there was a rapid return to more temperate conditions.

The final Würm glaciation was a period of constantly fluctuating climatic change, with several episodes of more temperate climate in northern latitudes. This particular glaciation served as a backdrop for the spread of anatomically modern Homo sapiens from the African tropics to all parts of the Old World and into the Americas. Between 25,000 and 15,000 years ago, Northern Eurasia's climate was intensely cold. A series of Stone Age gatherer-hunter cultures evolved both on the open tundra and in the sheltered river valleys of southwestern France and northern Spain, cultures famous for their antler and bond artifacts and artwork.

The world's geography was radically different 20,000 years ago. These differences had a major impact on human prehistory. One could walk from Siberia to Alaska across a flat, low-lying plain, the Bering Land Bridge. This was the route which most humans first reached the Americas some time before 12,000 years ago. The low-lying coastal zones of Southeast Asia were far more extensive 15,000 years ago than they are now, and they supported a thriving population of Stone Age gatherer-hunters. The fluctuating distributions of vegetational zones also affected the pattern of human settlement and the course of human history.

From a bioarchaeological perspective, the major climatic events of the past 1.5 million years provide a broad framework for a relative chronology of human culture. Although few human beings lived on or very close to the great ice sheets that covered so much of the northern hemisphere, they did live in regions affected by geological phenomena associated with the ice sheets: coastal areas, lakes, and river floodplains. When human artifacts are found in direct association with Pleistocene geological features of this type, it is sometimes possible to tie bioarchaeology to the relative chronology of Pleistocene events evident in the geological strata. Using sophisticated botanical methods such as pollen analysis, it is often possible to reconstruct local environments during the Pleistocene with remarkable precision. Many early gatherer-hunter bands camped on the shores of Pleistocene lakes that are now dry. The sealed deposits of these lakes are rich in organic materials that provide a wealth of information on the environment at the time the site was occupied. Millions of tiny fossil pollen grains from the trees and undergrowth that once grew near the lake are preserved in the lake filling. These pollen grains are highly distinctive and readily identified, because each tree or grass species has a different seed form. By taking samples from the lake deposits, it is possible to reconstruct the vegetation around a Pleistocene lake by identifying and counting the fossil pollens. This technique is called palynology and is the science of pollen analysis. It is the only means of gaining an accurate picture of prehistoric environments in any detail. For example, pollen samples have shown how gatherer-hunters living in Central Africa 50,000 years ago were systematically utilizing dense rain forests.

The relative chronology of the Pleistocene provides a general framework for the major events of prehistory. This framework becomes much more accurate after 100,000 BP when many more bioarchaeological sites are found near lakes and other localities, and pollen analysis can be used to study vegetational and environmental changes.

Laboratory Activities

Laboratory Activity 1. Discussion of comparative geological dating techniques

Identify and describe the specific strengths and limitations of the various geological dating approaches applied to materials from the following time frames. Be prepared to discuss your answers in lab.

Era	Period	Epoch	Millions of Years B.P.	Major Dating Methods Available
Cenozoic	Tertiary	Paleocene	53–66	
		Eocene	37–54	
		Oligocene	25–38	
		Miocene	5–26	
		Pliocene	1.8–6	
	Quarternary	Pleistocene	0.01–1.9	
		Holocene		

Laboratory Activity 2. Bioarchaeological reenactments and reconstructions

In this part of the laboratory, you will need to travel to the field site.

a. Students will divide into three or four groups at the field site where you are expected to survey the surface of a bioarchaeological simulation of an abandoned Upper Paleolithic shelter. Drawings should be made of these field sites.

b. From these noninvasive observations, each group will note the position and description of any osteological or artifactual remains from the site, and map the site.

c. Then students will work together to reconstruct an Upper Paleolithic shelter using the local materials available.

d. Use your pre-lab model as a guide and work collaboratively with your teammates.

e. Once you have constructed your shelter, sit or lay in it and take note of the experience.

f. Map out your site, draw your shelter, and report on its efficacy as part of your HOMEWORK assignment.

NOTE! You should prepare TWO layout drawings: one drawing of the site you encounter and any bioarchaeological materials still on the site and one drawing of the shelter you construct.

Grid for Diagramming Shelters and Bioarchaeological Field Site

Post-Lab Assignments

Diagram and map your Upper Paleolithic shelter made at the field site. Type a one-page report on the shelter you constructed at the field site including such information as:

a. Construction materials used, source, limitations

b. Overall structure of shelter (number of entrances/exits, shape of walls)

c. Number of people accommodated inside of shelter

d. Ambient shelter temperature changes with habitation

e. Comfort level of shelter (noise level, presence of resident insects, light levels)

f. Durability of shelter, ability to withstand wind, rain, cold, etc.

g. Location of hearth, proximity to sleeping areas, ventilation issues

h. Proximity of structure to water

i. Levelness of structure floor

j. Potential for expansion of the shelter, proximity to other shelters

OVERNIGHT AT YOUR SHELTER

If you are interested in intensifying your experiences in the shelter you've made, please sign up for this extra credit opportunity with your TA. A list of these students will be provided to the campus police. Weather permitting, interested students will be permitted to spend 12 hours nonstop at their shelter in an effort to replicate the Pleistocene experience. During this time, no electronic equipment, books, or supplemental foods will be permitted. Students will take notes of their experience in and around the shelters. Credit will only be given for those spending the entire 12 hours in residence, under the conditions described.

LAB 10

Human Migration, Microevolution, and Biocultural Variability

OBJECTIVES

- Simulated biocultural implications of migration
- Population affinity trees
- Reconstructing modern human origins

Human biodiversity is a major research interest of many anthropologists, particularly human biologists. The interpretation of the molecular genetics of modern humanity is greatly aided by knowledge of our historic migrations, an awareness of our deep genealogies, and an emerging understanding of the biological consequences of our rich and diverse cultural systems. In fact, it would be extremely difficult to make much sense out of our current molecular diversity without reference to humanity's evolutionary and ecological heritage. These data, when integrated, continue to provide the most meaningful context for evaluating the population meaning of human molecular genetics. These data also provide an independent set of criteria for determining the group significance, if any, of observed genotypic and phenotypic variations. In this lab students will retrace the genetic reshaping and cultural transformations in fissured subgroups of an originally homogenous population as a result of their migrations and unique biohistories. After seven generations of change they will reconvene and explore the genetic and nongenetic changes they have been subjected to. This lab integrates many of the materials presented in previous aspects of the course and serves as a synthesis of the core concepts in biological anthropology.

Purpose of This Laboratory

This laboratory is primarily a simulation exercise to acquaint you with the major concepts of population biology. These concepts are central to biological anthropology and allow scientists to develop testable hypotheses about how small groups can change rapidly in biological and cultural composition over a few generations. You will experience these changes and will be able to comparatively assess the experiences of your own group to that of others.

Goals and Objectives

The goal of this lab is to expose students to the role of migration and biohistory in genetically reshaping and culturally transforming an originally homozygous group.

Key Terms and Topics

transhumance, optimal phenotypes, heredity and environment, human microevolution and biodiversity, effects of migration on genetic composition

Pre-Lab Assignments

1. Review the background materials on reconstructing past human migrations from environmental and genetic data and human biodiversity (below).

2. Study the field site map; know the various migration points and study your group's proposed movements, disease and accident exposures, and interactions with other groups.

Background on Human Biodiversity

Great basic similarity exists among all humans. All contemporary humans are members of a common yet highly variable subspecies (=biological race). As a population, we are classified taxonomically as *Homo sapiens sapiens,* in spite of our notable biodiversity. It is this extensive variation that enhances our biological and behavioral flexibility. Our great biodiversity is also considered to be a significant buffer against rapid extinction. When humanity is confronted with new environmental challenges (for example, a new infectious disease such as the HIVs), inherent human biodiversity may ensure that at least some members will survive the challenge and carry on the species.

Subdividing humanity into "racial categories" ignores the tremendous genetic heterogeneity within these groupings. Most "racial groups" are linked biologically on the basis of a few general phenotypic characteristics (such as hair form, eye shape, skin color) whose genetic basis is not yet known. So, while such groupings may seem to be natural categories, in fact, they are biologically superficial, frequently of limited biomedical value, and sometimes irrelevant to understanding the genetics of a particular disease process. Broad categories such as mongoloids, caucasoids, and negroids, for example, are meaningless in understanding the nuances of human genetic diversity because each of these "classic" groupings phenotypically and genotypically overlaps with the others.

In this lab students will form groups of four that will function as a "tribe." As students move (migrate) from station to station they will undergo diverse evolutionary processes. As a result, the group will be transformed over the course of seven generations of movement and exposure to differential selection and drift. At the conclusion of the migratory process, each "tribe" will return to its home base (the Bioanthropology Teaching Lab) and discuss the changes that occurred as a result of their unique group histories. These changes will then be used to evaluate the plausibility of the various scientific theories proposed to explain the origins of modern humans.

Laboratory Activities

Laboratory Activity 1. Past human migrations

Human migration is a salient part of human history. Everything from our anatomy to our cultures suggests that transhumance has been an ancient part of the human story. Using the maps provided by your instructor, please do the following:

1. Diagram at least three well-documented human migration patterns that have occurred within the last 100,000 years.
2. Indicate the estimated time of each migration.
3. Identify the anticipated adaptive biobehavioral consequences of each migration on the descendants of the original immigrants.
4. Discuss your selections in lab with the entire class. This discussion is in preparation for the major laboratory activity (on the next page).

Laboratory Activity 2. Geographical migrations and genetic and cultural change simulation

Geographic distances are often taken as an approximation of the length of migratory movements. Indeed, geographical distance does explain a substantial part of the genetic diversity of human populations. However, in most instances, straight line or great-circle distances between populations only give a crude estimate of the real "distance" between them. The best way to measure the true traveling distance is to follow the path used by walking migrants. This path is influenced, among other things, by the topography and the vegetation of the terrain. Conditions such as topography, continental contours, vegetation, and hydrology need to be factored into our assessments of "distance" to give a better prediction of the true degree of geographical separation between groups.

1. Students will group themselves into "tribes" of six individuals. Each individual will receive one red gene, one blue gene, one green gene, and one yellow gene.

2. Each member of the "tribe" will receive his or her initial cultural identity and will follow the migration guides for that tribe.

3. Students will walk through this guide, site by site, and at each site they will open an envelope with instructions for an event at that site.

4. Groups should spend exactly 10 minutes at each site, no more and no less, otherwise they will be off schedule for the next "appointment with microevolution."

5. These site instructions will explain what the group is being subjected to at that particular site and the resulting genetic and cultural repercussions.

6. Members of the group will then modify their original cultural identities and genetic composition as required by the changing circumstances.

7. After these modifications, surviving members of the group will "reproduce" by genetically replicating themselves from the group's stash of extra genes.

8. This represents a new generation; old genes will "die off" and be replaced by "new genes" that reflect the microevolutionary events of the previous generation.

9. At times each "tribe" will encounter opportunities for genetic drift, directional selection, diversifying selection, balancing selection, gene flow, assertive mating, etc.

10. However, since each group will experience these microevolutionary forces at different times in their tribe's history, at differing intensities and durations, and in response to different specific events, the effects on the tribe's genetic composition will vary from one group to the next. At each generation, members of each tribe will also experience cultural change. This also needs to be documented by the tribe's historian.

11. After seven generations of change, "tribes" will return to home base, complete the data report sheets entitled "Migration Effects," and discuss the transformations that ensued within the class as a whole.

12. These changes will then be compared with the diversity present among contemporary humans and the various hypotheses prevalent to account for such diversity will be evaluated.

13. Specifically we will discuss your group's data in light of the various candelabra and lattice models of modern human origins.

Key to the Major Field Migration Sites:
(at the University of Maryland, College Park, MD)

A.	East African Woods	Woods Hall
B.	Nile Delta	Bottom of Fountain
C.	Black Forrest	Between Holzapfel & Simmons
D.	Stonehenge	Stone Sculptures
E.	Testudo Terraces	Testudo
F.	Straits of McKeldin	Paths behind McKeldin
G.	Walls of Jericho	Wall in front of Administration Bldg.
H.	Steppes of Key	Key Hall steps
I.	Nile Headwaters	Sundial
J.	Volcano Mount	Mary Mount Hall
K.	Gardens of Babylon	Woods Courtyard

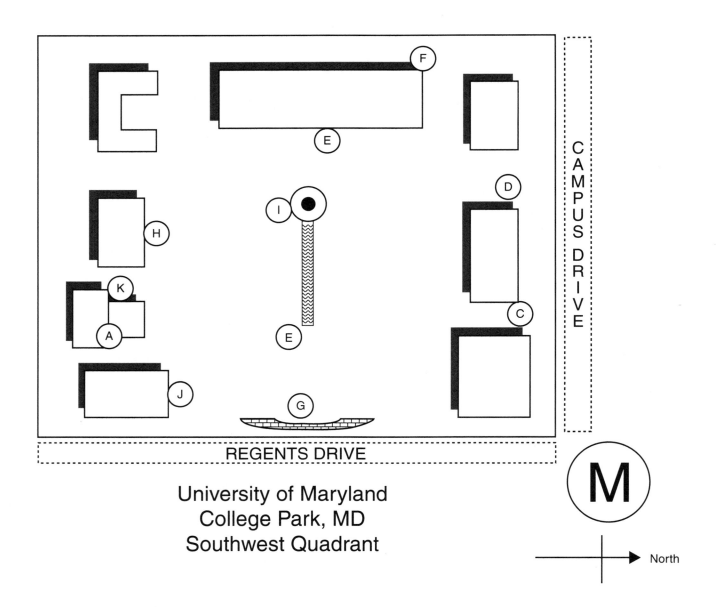

University of Maryland
College Park, MD
Southwest Quadrant

Migration Effects Data Report Sheets

Generation 1

Starting Gene Frequencies

RED   GREEN   BLUE   YELLOW

____   ____   ____   ____

Site and events description

_____

_____

_____

_____

Effects on individuals and group: _____

_____

_____

ADDITIONAL COMMENTS:

Generation 2

New Gene Frequencies

RED   GREEN   BLUE   YELLOW

____   ____   ____   ____

Site and events description

_____

_____

_____

_____

Effects on individuals and group: _____

_____

_____

ADDITIONAL COMMENTS:

Generation 3

New Gene Frequencies

RED   GREEN   BLUE   YELLOW

_____   _____   _____   _____

Site and events description

_____

_____

_____

_____

Effects on individuals and group: _____

_____

_____

ADDITIONAL COMMENTS:

Generation 4

New Gene Frequencies

RED   GREEN   BLUE   YELLOW

_____   _____   _____   _____

Site and events description

_____

_____

_____

_____

Effects on individuals and group: _____

_____

_____

ADDITIONAL COMMENTS:

Generation 5

New Gene Frequencies

RED   GREEN   BLUE   YELLOW

____   ____   ____   ____

Site and events description

_____

_____

_____

_____

Effects on individuals and group: _____

_____

_____

ADDITIONAL COMMENTS:

Generation 6

New Gene Frequencies

RED   GREEN   BLUE   YELLOW

____   ____   ____   ____

Site and events description

_____

_____

_____

_____

_____

Effects on individuals and group: _____

_____

ADDITIONAL COMMENTS:

Generation 7

Final Gene Frequencies

Site and events description

RED   GREEN   BLUE   YELLOW

_____   _____   _____   _____

_____

_____

_____

_____

Effects on individuals and group: _____

_____

_____

ADDITIONAL COMMENTS:

Summary:

_____

_____

_____

_____

_____

_____

_____

_____

_____

_____

_____

Laboratory Activity 3

Plot the changes in gene frequencies observed within your group over seven generations of migration and variable directional and stochastic (random) events.

LEGEND

☐ Red Gene Freq.

☐ Green Gene Freq.

☐ Blue Gene Freq.

☐ Yellow Gene Freq.

Which event had the biggest impact of specific gene frequencies? Why? _____

_____

_____

_____

Perform the chi-square test to determine if these gene frequency differences after seven generations of migration are statistically significant.

Laboratory Activity 4. Analysis of genetic changes and discussion of candelabra and lattice models of modern human origins

After completing seven generations of genetic and cultural change, all tribes should reunite at the Bioanthropology Teaching Lab. Here group stories will be exchanged and the resulting biocultural changes analyzed. Students should be prepared to discuss their group's modifications within the context of the various candelabra (Out of Africa, Multiregional Evolution) hypotheses as well as the lattice model of modern human origins.

QUESTION: What magnitude of genetic change is possible within seven generations? Is this change "microevolution"?

QUESTION: How do cultural and environmental factors influence group gene frequencies? What does this mean for understanding human adaptability and biodiversity?

QUESTION: Using the form provided, plot the changes in gene frequencies observed within your group over seven generations of migration and variable directional and stochastic events; how do your tribe's changes compare with those of the entire class?

QUESTION: Which events had the biggest impact on specific gene frequencies and why? Can you quantify the impact of specific cultural and environmental events?

QUESTION: Perform the chi-square test to determine if these gene frequency differences after seven generations of change are statistically significant. Were these changes bioanthropologically significant?

QUESTION: How does your tribe's story relate to the current theories on modern human origins?

QUESTION: Contrast and critique these theories given your migration/gene change experience. Which of the theories seem more plausible in light of your experience?

Developing Explanatory Models for Human Genetic and Cultural Change Over Time Using the Geography of the Duffy Blood Group Alleles

Consider the effects of migration, gene flow, genetic drift, founder effect, directional selection, stabilizing selection, diversifying selection mutation, recombination, and other aspects of microevolution.

QUESTION: Briefly, what is your explanation for the differences in the Fy^a gene frequencies in (West) Africa and in the USA?

QUESTION: What demographic factors do you think might have contributed to the geographical variation (or lack of) in the gene frequencies of the Fy^a allele?

QUESTION: What environmental (ecological) factors may have also influenced frequencies?

QUESTION: What are the imbedded assumptions of your explanatory model?

QUESTION: What are your model's strengths and limitations?

Be sure to turn in this completed form to your TA before you begin the next lab!

Post-Lab Assignments

The Duffy Blood Group alleles have been carefully studied in many human groups worldwide. Given what you have learned about the alleles associated with this blood group system, interpret the chart presented below. Develop a plausible explanatory model for the pattern observed in the frequencies of the *Fy* allele. What factors would you hypothesize have contributed to the geographical variation (or lack of) in the gene frequencies of the *Fy* allele? What unidentified factors may have also influenced frequencies? What are the assumptions of your explanatory model? What are your model's strengths and limitations? Type your answers on two pages and submit these as a homework assignment. Be sure to address each question posed.

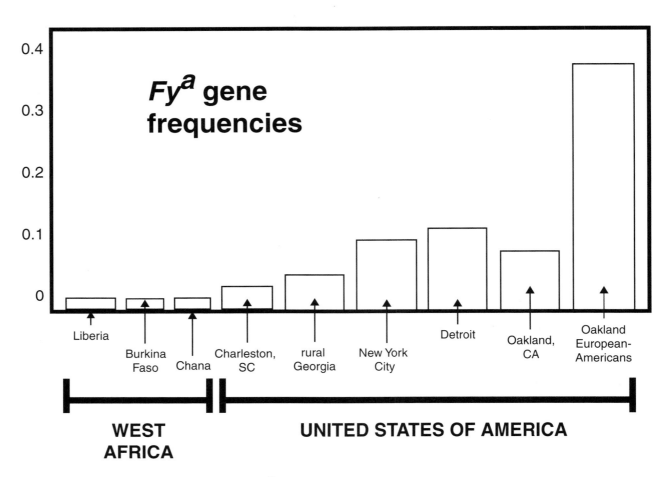

Frequencies of the *Fy^a* (Duffy Blood Group) allele among various Africans and African Americans

LAB

11

The Genus *Homo* and the Evolution of Human Cognition

OBJECTIVES

- Cognition and physiology: hypothesis testing
- Upper Paleolithic artistic expression
- The evolution of the human brain, language, cognition, and abstract reasoning

As biocultural organisms, humans rely upon both culture and human biology to survive, reproduce, and evolve. The combination of biological and cultural strategies has allowed humans greater flexibility and enhanced our potential to evolve to the highly adaptive species seen today. In this laboratory, students will have an opportunity to explore several aspects of cognition. Together we will test the hypothesis that physical position influences mental state, we will re-create classical Upper Paleolithic and Neolithic artwork, and we will discuss some of the newest advances in neuroanatomy and cognition.

Purpose of This Laboratory

One of the areas that biological anthropologists tend to be particularly good at is linking structure to function. The set of exercises in this laboratory section provide you with an opportunity to test a hypothesis that suggests that physical position influences physiological function. Through your reenactments of the artistic activities of our Upper Paleolithic ancestors, you will have an opportunity to imagine the cognitive changes they may have experienced. This will greatly facilitate our review of what is currently surmised about the evolution of the human brain, language, self-consciousness, and abstract reasoning.

Goals and Objectives

In this lab, students will undertake three major activities. The first activity will be to test a hypothesis proposed by Dr. Felicitas D. Goodman, a linguistic anthropologist, who became very interested in the cross-cultural physiological effects of trance positions depicted in the archaeological record. Students will reenact these positions and evaluate the cognitive effects, if any, of the positions during a brief trance. In the second half of the laboratory, students will have an opportunity to re-create in lab some of the classical Upper Paleolithic and early Neolithic artwork of diverse human groups. As a third activity, we will explore the neuroanatomy of the human brain and discuss some of the latest developments in cognitive sciences as they relate to evolution and language development.

Key Terms and Topics

cognition, self-awareness, icon, gross anatomy, culture transmission, creativity and intelligence, cerebral laterality, language areas of the cortex, evolution of the human brain

Pre-Lab Assignments

(complete before the beginning of lab)

1. Review the anatomy of the human brain. Which areas are considered responsible for speech, cognition, and moral values?

2. What is a trance? How can it be induced and what happens physiologically when one is in a trance?

3. Identify three symbols from modern human cultures. What do these abstractions mean? How are symbols able to evoke strong emotional responses in us?

4. Review the background material on human cognition and be prepared to incorporate this information into this lab's experiments

Laboratory Activities

Laboratory Activity 1: Re-creation and cognitive assessments of classical human trance position from prehistory and history

Dr. Goodman hypothesized that physical position has an effect on cognition. She believes that the position seen in various archaeological icons actually induced a specific physiological state. We will briefly test this hypothesis in an effort to understand the evolution of the human brain. Our protocol is as follows:

- Each student will try to reproduce four trance positions from the archaeological record for approximately 15 minutes each, following the diagrams provided by your TA.
- The positions you take may be on the floor, on a chair, or standing.
- Each of the positions are positions commonly observed in icons and cave drawings from the Neolithic period.
- As students stand in a circle, the repeating beat of a drum will help you enter a very light trance state.
- During this time you will maintain your position and become very conscious of your physiological and cognitive states.
- After 15 minutes, the drumming will cease and you will come out of the light trance.
- After each trance, each student should quickly write down what he or she experienced.
- Experiences will then be collated and discussed as a group.
- Dr. Goodman's hypothesis will be critiqued as we test her hypothesis.
- If our data reject the null hypothesis (no change with trance position), we will consider the alternative hypotheses.

Laboratory Activity 2: Re-creation of classical Upper Paleolithic and early Neolithic artwork of diverse human groups

In this part of the lab, students will have an opportunity to reproduce some of the art techniques used by our remote ancestors in the Upper Paleolithic and early Neolithic. This is a "free-form" part of the lab; students can work with clay, a special Paleolithic paint mixture, and charcoal. Students may try the traditional technique of mixing mouth ground charcoal with saliva and spitting it over a hand (or other object) onto the "canvas"—usually a cave wall—to create a signature hand print. Red ochre can be used in the same fashion. Students may also wish to try drawing some of the animals of the Pleistocene using sticks, twigs, leaves, and other primitive materials. Of course, body painting is another appropriate option!

- Students will select two to three different mediums to work with during this part of the lab.
- Conceptualize your end product by making mental or actual line drawings, prepare your materials, and begin application.
- In the case of charcoal and red ochre, mix these with your own saliva and spray them onto the "cave" wall using the classical Stone Age techniques (your TA can show you how).

    Available media for these activities include clay, paints mixed with (vegetable) fats, various plant dyes, etc.

Laboratory Activity 3: Discussion of the evolution of the human brain, language, cognition, abstract reasoning, manipulation of information, future planning, etc.

During this part of the lab, students will look at gross anatomy of human brains and discuss the acquisition and transmission of language. Using the half-brain diagram in the Lab Notebook and the full brain diagram in Appendix 1 of your text, identify the following areas listed by your TA. These will include, but are not limited to:

- Frontal lobe
- Olfactory bulb
- Optic nerve
- Hippocampus
- Brain stem

Background on Human Cognition

Cultural views define human existence and the dominant role of culture separates *Homo sapiens sapiens* from the other hominids. Although chimpanzees and bonobos (*Pan* spp.) exhibit some cultural norms such as tool use, human manipulation of the environment occurs at a much larger, more intense, more consistent, and more intricate scale. The knowledge of self-cognition remains a basic building block of culture, and is hence a core issue in anthropology.

It is not known exactly when modern humans gained this knowledge of self. Anthropologists can only make educated guesses using artifacts, knowledge of contemporary human behavior patterns, neurological reconstructions of the hominid brain, etc. The most defining bioanthropological evidence suggesting cognition is artistic creations. When someone creates a piece of art, such as cave paintings, the person is often making an individualistic expression of commonly held group values. The artist demonstrates a knowledge of him or herself as well as that of the surrounding world. Many cave paintings and other pieces of early art deal with spiritual matters. Sometimes specific rituals are depicted, while at other times, the artwork seems to be representations of the concept of a Creator-God. At other times, burial symbols are displayed. Such deliberate symbolic expression dignifies consciousness, preconception, and is strong evidence of cognition.

Most of our knowledge of the Upper Paleolithic comes from studies of European sites. Clearly there were similar changes in other parts of the world, but these have not yet been systematically examined. During this time period (Arignacian/Perigordian) and especially during the subsequent Magdalenean period, the artwork was particularly spectacular. The Altamira cave in northern Spain, for example, is filled with superb portrayals of bison in red and black that coincide with the natural bulges of the cave wall. We still do not know why such beautiful artwork was produced there. It could have been religious, ritualistic, magical, a form of visual communication, or just art for the sake of beauty. During this time period, we also find evidence of beautiful bone beads, shell and stone pendants, rock art, body art, and decorated clothing. Decorated stone tools were also made along with realistic animal carvings and sculptured figurines.

REPORT FORM
CRITICAL ASSESSMENT OF THE GOODMAN HYPOTHESIS

TRANCE POSITION 1
Basic Null Hypothesis: Trance position 1 does not produce any specific physiological response.

BASELINE PHYSIOLOGICAL STATE

DESCRIPTION OF TRANCE POSITION

LOCATION OF TESTING SITE

DURATION OF HYPOTHESIS TESTING

COGNITIVE ASSESSMENT

PHYSIOLOGICAL ASSESSMENT

TESTED NULL HYPOTHESIS: Given the time and location of testing, trance position 1 does not produce any specific physiological response.

REJECT   ACCEPT

IF REJECTED, PROPOSE AN ALTERNATIVE HYPOTHESIS BASED UPON YOUR PERSONAL EXPERIENCE AND GROUP OBSERVATIONS

REPORT FORM
CRITICAL ASSESSMENT OF THE GOODMAN HYPOTHESIS

TRANCE POSITION 2

Basic Null Hypothesis: Trance position 2 does not produce any specific physiological response.

BASELINE PHYSIOLOGICAL STATE

DESCRIPTION OF TRANCE POSITION

LOCATION OF TESTING SITE

DURATION OF HYPOTHESIS TESTING

COGNITIVE ASSESSMENT

PHYSIOLOGICAL ASSESSMENT

TESTED NULL HYPOTHESIS: Given the time and location of testing, trance position 2 does not produce any specific physiological response.

REJECT   ACCEPT

IF REJECTED, PROPOSE AN ALTERNATIVE HYPOTHESIS BASED UPON YOUR PERSONAL EXPERIENCE AND GROUP OBSERVATIONS

REPORT FORM
CRITICAL ASSESSMENT OF THE GOODMAN HYPOTHESIS

TRANCE POSITION 3

Basic Null Hypothesis: Trance position 3 does not produce any specific physiological response.

BASELINE PHYSIOLOGICAL STATE

DESCRIPTION OF TRANCE POSITION

LOCATION OF TESTING SITE

DURATION OF HYPOTHESIS TESTING

COGNITIVE ASSESSMENT

PHYSIOLOGICAL ASSESSMENT

TESTED NULL HYPOTHESIS: Given the time and location of testing, trance position 3 does not produce any specific physiological response.

REJECT   ACCEPT

IF REJECTED, PROPOSE AN ALTERNATIVE HYPOTHESIS BASED UPON YOUR PERSONAL EXPERIENCE AND GROUP OBSERVATIONS

Post-Lab Assignments

(due at the beginning of the next lab period)

- Complete the report forms entitled "Critical Assessment of the Goodman Hypothesis."
- Conduct a tool/faunal assemblage and activity analysis of a cave site.

Collect your three minibags of soil and artifacts from a cave site (provided by your TA).

a. Note the location from which your bioarchaeological samples were taken from the reference map below.

b. Use the locations of your samples to help you analyze the artifacts carefully.

c. Clean, describe (quantitatively and qualitatively), and label all recovered materials in the sample bags.

d. Keep detailed notes on your assessments (fill out the sheets in your Lab Manual) and be prepared to add your observations to those of your classmates in reconstructing the biohistory of this cave site.

e. Fill out the inventory and use/behavior assessment reports on your cave site tool/faunal assemblages.

f. Be prepared to discuss (and defend) your interpretation of the cave site.

GENERAL MAP OF THE MYSTERY CAVE SITE

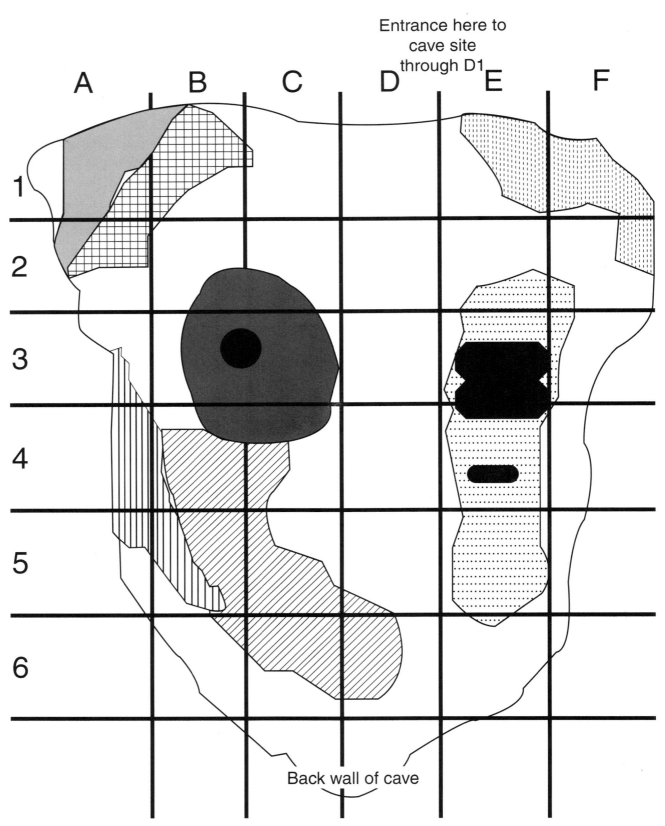

Entrance here to cave site through D1

Back wall of cave

LAB 12

Human Osteology

- Skeletal biology
- Forensic anthropology

Purpose of This Laboratory

The study of the human skeleton is a core theme in biological anthropology. Knowledge of human skeletal biology allows biological anthropologists to be able to determine many aspects of an unknown skeleton, including age, sex, physical stresses during the individual's life, likely geographical ancestral origins, and other important identifying variables. Understanding human skeletal biology is an important part of the discipline.

Goals and Objectives

The purpose of this lab is to learn the terminology of skeletal biology and the identification of human bones. We will also determine the structure and function of bones.

Pre-Lab Assignments

1. List three functions of bone.

2. Review the names of the bones of the skeleton as shown in the diagram in your lab. What are the four *distal* bones of the arm and the leg?

3. What kind of information might be obtained from studying muscle attachments on bones?

Laboratory Activities

Laboratory Activity 1. Examine the displays of skeletal material around the lab and answer the following questions

General Bone Morphology Human vs. Nonhuman Remains

- For the bones on display at this station, list the names of the bones and indicate if they are human and or nonhuman. Use the articulated skeletons for comparison.
- Compare the unknown vertebra to the three labeled vertebrae. Is it cervical thoracic or lumbar?
- Are the femur, scapula, and ulna from the right or left side?
- What part of the skeleton is the bone labeled D from?

Age

- Based on the dental eruption charts, what is the approximate age of the juvenile mandible on display?
- What is the approximate age of the adult rib using the sternal rib morphology?
- What is the approximate age of the adult os coxae based on the pubic symphysis?

Sex

- Compare the unknown skull to the labeled male and female skulls. Is it male or female? Use the charts in the lab to help you.
- Compare the unknown os coxa to the labeled male and female os coxa. Is it male or female? Use the charts in the lab to help you.

Trauma and Pathology

- List at least five types of pathologies that can affect the skeleton.
- Describe the appearance of a fracture in skeletal material.

Glossary of Position and Movement

anatomical position—face forward, arms at the side with palms of hand facing forward; the directional terms (anterior, poster, etc.) refer to the body or skeleton in this position.
anterior—in front
distal—away from the trunk or head
extension—movement of a limb, or part of a limb away from the body
flexion—bending of a joint
inferior—lower; below
lateral—away from the midline
medial—toward the midline
posterior—back; behind
proximal—close to the torso or head
superior—upper, above

Laboratory Activity 2. Description of human remains

The class will divide into two groups and will work on the skeletal remains of a single individual. Lay out the disarticulated human skeleton in anatomical position. You may use the articulated skeletons as a guideline. Be careful to put the bones on the correct side. Make an inventory of the bones that are present and absent. Also, note if the bones are complete and their general condition.

Use the reference charts to determine age and sex of the individual. These charts are from the *Standards for Data Collection from Human Skeletal Remains* (Buiksta & Ubelaker, eds.). Be sure to note in detail the results of your analysis and your final conclusions.

Document any pathological conditions, anomalies (such as extra teeth, fusion of two bones, etc.), or trauma. You should go over each part of the skeleton carefully. You may divide the bones up among group members and share your data.

Post-Lab Assignment

Write a description of the skeleton you worked with in the lab (2-3 pages). This should include a general description of the material, the results of your age and sex analysis (including methodology), and any other information about pathologies or anomalies that you documented.

*What age and sex?
*What is missing?
*Anything missing?
*Any possible pathologies?

*Study Quiz
next Friday

Vertebral
C - 7
T - 12
L - 5 ✓

vertebra not collapsed too much
ribs not too deep
no picures on pelvis
a lot of cartilage on ribs

Male
30 (±5 years)

pelvis is narrower

MISS
○ clavicle
○ cranium
● metatarsals
○ metacarpals
● phalanges

*do not use skull to determine male or female

pathology
○ hole in sternum
○ benign deformaty (genetic condition)
● sternum foramen is name

Glossary

Adaptation In the broadest sense, the process by which organisms adapt to current environmental conditions. In anthropological genetics, a heritable component of the phenotype which confers an advantage in survival and reproductive success. In evolutionary biology, any structure, physiological process, or behavioral pattern that bestows upon an organism greater fitness or ability to survive and to reproduce in comparison with other members of the same species. Also, the evolutionary process leading to the formation of such a trait.

Adaptive Refers to any trait, anatomical, physiological, or behavioral, that arose by the process of adaptation.

Adaptive radiation The process of evolution in which species multiply, diverge into different ecological niches, and come to occupy the same or at least overlapping ranges (e.g., Darwin's finches, predators on different kinds of prey, occupants of different habitats).

Age of Mammals The Cenozoic Era, which spans the last 65 million years of earth's history.

Allele One of several forms of the same gene capable of segregating as a Mendelian unit. The alleles presumably arise by mutation of the DNA sequence.

Allele frequency The proportion of individuals in a population carrying a particular allele.

Allopatric speciation The process of speciation associated with or resulting from geographic isolation.

Analogous Refers to the similarity of form or structure between two species that do not share such similarities with their nearest common ancestor. The similarity in structure evolved independently in the two species and is due to convergent evolution.

Anthropoid A member of the suborder Anthropoidea (higher primates), including Old and New World monkeys, apes, and humans; sometimes used to describe just the apes.

Anthropometry The science of the measurement of the size, weight, and proportions of the human body.

Antibody A protein (an immunoglobin) produced in response to an antigenic stimulus with the ability to bind specifically to the antigen.

Antigen A molecule, often a cell surface protein, that is capable of allocating or inducing the formation of antibodies.

Antisocial factor Any selective pressure that has a tendency to inhibit or to reverse social evolution.

Arboreal Refers to any organism living mainly in the trees.

Arboreal quadrupeds Animals that use all four limbs in walking and running on tree limbs.

Arboreal theory A theory subscribing to the concept that most of the cranial and postcranial trends found in primates initially evolved as adaptations for life in the trees.

Australopithecine A member of the subfamily Australopithecine; a group of early hominids belonging to the genus

Australopithecus; primitive forms that lived during the Pleistocene Epoch and were ancestral to modern humans (genus *Homo*). Specifically, australopithecines lived in East and South Africa during the Plio-Pleistocene and possessed postures and dentition similar to those of modern men but brains not much larger than those of modern apes. Pertaining to the "man-apes."

Balanced polymorphism   The maintenance of genetic polymorphism in a population by natural selection.

Bergmann's rule   A general rule in zoology that animals living in cold climates tend to be larger than closely related species living in warm climates. This results in a lower surface-area-to-volume ratio and thus reduces heat loss in colder climates; also loosely applicable to human populations.

Brachial index   The ratio of the length of the forearm (radius) divided by the length of the upper arm (humerus) $\times$ 100.

Brachiation   Arboreal locomotion in which the animal progresses through the branches by using only the forelimbs in a hand over hand fashion.

Catarrhine   A member of the infraorder Catarrhini, Old World anthropoids including monkeys, apes, and humans.

Ceboid   A member of the superfamily Ceboidea (living New World primates).

Cercopithcid   A member of the Cercopithecidae, the family of Old World Monkeys including both living and extinct members of the late Miocene through the present.

Cercopithecine   A member of the Cercopithecinae, the subfamily of the Old World Monkeys characterized by cheek pouches.

Character convergence   The process by which two newly evolved species interact such that one or both converges in one or more traits toward the other (contrast with character displacement).

Character displacement   The process by which two newly evolved species interact so as to cause one or both of them to diverge still further in evolution (contrast with character convergence).

Chromosomal aberration   Any change occurring as the result of duplication, deletion, or rearrangement of chromosomal material.

Chromosomal polymorphism   Alternate structures or arrangements of a chromosome carried by members of a population.

Chromosome   A threadlike structure containing genetic information arranged in a linear sequence. In eukaryotes, a chromosome consists of a DNA molecule complexed with RNA and proteins.

Clade   In the narrow sense, a group or set of species descended from a single common ancestral species. Sometimes used more as a set of related species, from which some descendants are excluded. A clade may be represented by a distinct branch in phylogenetic tree (contrast with evolutionary grade).

Cladism   Classification by shared derived characters; also called phylogenic systematics.

Cladistic   Pertaining to branching patterns; a cladistic analysis classifies organisms on the basis of the historical sequences by which they diverged from common ancestors.

Cladogram   Branching tree diagram or phylogenetic tree used to represent phyletic relationships—the splitting of species and groups of species through evolutionary time. Also called a cladistic tree.

Cline   A pattern or gradient of gradual genetic (genotypic or phenotypic) change in a population distributed over its geographic range.

Codominance   Condition in which the phenotypic effects of gene alleles at the same locus are fully and simultaneously expressed in the heterozygote.

Codon   A triplet of bases in a DNA or RNA molecule which specifies or codes for the formation of a single amino acid.

Coefficient of kinship   Symbolized by FIJ or fIJ, the probability that a pair of alleles drawn at random from the same locus on two individuals are identical by virtue of common descent. Also called the coefficient of consanguinity.

Coefficient of relationship   Also known as the degree of relatedness, symbolized by r. The coefficient of relationship is the fraction of identical genes by virtue of common descent between two individuals.

Coefficient of selection   A measurement of the reproductive disadvantage of a given genotype in a population. If for genotype aa, only 99 or 100 individuals reproduce, then the selection coefficient (s) is 0.1.

Coefficient of variation   The statistical measure of variability that is independent of size.

Coefficient of variation (C.V.)   The standard deviation divided by the mean, multiplied by 100. C.V. $= 100 \times (s / x)$.

Colobine   A member of Colobinae; leaf eating monkeys of the subfamily of Old World monkeys.

Consanguine   Related by a common ancestor within the previous few generations.

Crossing over   The exchange of chromosomal material between homologous chromosomes by breakage and reunion of portions of the chromosomes during meiosis (sexual reproduction). The exchange of material between nonsister chromatid during meiosis introduces variation and is the basis of genetic recombination.

Cytoplasmin inheritance   Non-Mendelian inheritance involving genetic information transmitted by self-replicating cytoplasmin organelles (mitochondria, chloroplasts, etc.).

Darwinism   The theory of evolution by natural selection, as originally propounded by Charles Darwin. The modern version of this theory, often called neo-Darwinism, still recognizes natural selection as the central process of evolution.

Deme   A local randomly interbreeding population. The largest population unit that can be analyzed by simpler models of population genetics.

Demography   The rate of growth, the age structure of populations, and the processes that determine these properties.

Density dependence   The increase or decrease of the influence of physiological or environmental factors on population growth as the density of the population increases.

Deoxyribonucleic acid (DNA)   The primary carrier of genetic information. A macromolecule usually consisting of polynucleotide chains held together by hydrogen bonds, in which sugar residues are deoxyribose.

Derived character   The evolutionary later stage of a character, relative to its ancestral state; also called an apometry.

Diploid   A condition in which each chromosome exists in pairs; having two of each chromosome.

Directional selection   Selection that operates against one end of the range of variation in a population and tends to shift the entire population toward the opposite end over time.

Directional selection   A selective force that changes the frequency of an allele in a given direction, either toward fixation or toward elimination.

Discontinuous variation   Phenotypic data, falling into two or more distinct classes, which do not overlap.

Disruptive selection   Simultaneous selection for phenotypic extremes in a population, usually resulting in the production of two discontinuous strains. This type of selection may eventually result in two distinct populations or, in the extreme, to speciation.

Doliocephalic   Having a long, narrow skull. Measurements in humans are comparative between or within populations.

Encephalization quotient (EQ)   The measure of relative brain size; the brain weight is compared with that of the average living mammal of equal body weight.

Enculturation   The transmission of a particular culture, especially to the young members of a society.

Endemic   Restricted to a specific region or locality (i.e., endemic species).

Environment   The complex of geographic, climatic, and biotic factors in which an organism lives.

Environmentalism   In biology, the form of analysis that stresses the role of environmental influences over other influences (e.g., genetic) in the development of behavioral or biological traits.

Enzyme   A protein or complex of proteins that catalyzes a specific biochemical reaction.

Epigenesis   The developmental process by which the genotype is expressed as a phenotype.

Equilibrium   A condition of stasis, for example, population size or genetic composition. Also the value itself (of a population size, gene frequency) at which stasis occurs.

Evolution   In the broadest sense, any gradual change. Organic evolution is any genetic change (a change in gene frequencies within populations) in organisms from generation to generation. Such changes occur by the origin and subsequent alteration of allelic or genotypic frequencies from generation to generation within populations, by the alteration of the proportions of genetically differentiated populations of a species, or by changes in the numbers of species with different characteristics, and may result in altering the frequency of one or more traits within a higher taxon. The origin of plants and animals from preexisting types or descent with modifications.

Evolutionary biology   The collective disciplines of biology that treat the evolutionary process and the characteristics of populations of organisms. These disciplines integrate evolution, ecology, behavior, and systematics.

Evolutionary convergence   The independent acquisition of a particular trait or set of traits by two or more species through the process of evolution.

Evolutionary grade   The level of development in a particular structure, physiological process, or behavior occupied by a species or group of species in the context of evolution. This is not to be confused with the phylogeny of a group, which is the relationship of species by descent.

Evolutionary taxonomy System of taxonomy based upon both the branching pattern of evolution and the amount of evolutionary change occurring along each lineage.

Expressivity The degree or range to which a phenotype for a given trait is expressed.

Extranuclear inheritance Transmission of traits via genetic information contained in cytoplasmic organelles such as mitochondria and chloroplasts.

Familial trait A trait expressed by or transmitted through members of a family.

Fission track dating A method of dating rocks utilizing the radioactive decay of uranium-238 in the rocks by counting the number of spontaneously produced fission tracks.

Fitness A measure of the relative survival and reproductive success of a given individual or genotype over time. The average contribution of one allele or genotype to the next generation or to succeeding generations as compared with that of other alleles or genotypes in a population.

Fixation In population genetics, a condition in which all members of a population are homozygous for a given allele.

Foramen magnum The large hole in the base of the skull through which the spinal cord passes.

Formation In geology, a fundamental rock unit of a straitigraphic section at a given locality.

Founder effect A form of genetic drift which occurs via the establishment of a population by a small number of individuals whose genotypes carry only a fraction of the different kinds of alleles in the parental population. The genetic differentiation of an isolated population due to the fact that by chance alone its founders contained a set of genes statistically different from those of other populations.

Frequency distribution The array of numbers of individuals showing differing values of some variable quantity (e.g., the number of offspring of different ages in a population carrying a specific trait).

Gamete The specialized reproductive cell containing a haploid number of chromosomes.

Geological time units The geological time units of the era, period, epoch, and age corresponding to the time-stratigraphic units of erathem, system, series, and standard stage. These abstract units of time exist whether or not any rock units actually record the passage of that particular interval of time.

Gene The fundamental, functional, physical unit of heredity (a DNA sequence coding for a single polypeptide) whose existence can be confirmed by allelic variants which occupies a specific chromosomal locus. The basic unit of heredity.

Gene flow The gradual exchange of genes between two populations, brought about by dispersal of gametes or the migration of individuals. Also refers to the exchange of genes between different species (an extreme case referred to as hybridization).

Gene frequency The percentage of alleles of a given type in a population or the proportion of gene copies in a population for which an allele accounts. Statistically described as the probability of finding this allele when a gene is taken randomly from the population. See allele frequency.

Gene interaction Novel phenotypes produced by the interaction of alleles of different genes.

Gene pool The total of all genes possessed by reproductive members of a population, hence all the hereditary material in a population.

Genetic burden The average number of recessive lethal genes carried in a heterozygous condition by an individual in a population. Also called genetic load.

Genetic code The nucleotide triplets that code for the 20 amino acids or for the chain initiation or termination in the production of amino acid chains.

Genetic drift Random changes in the gene frequencies of two or more alleles within a population from generation to generation; most often observed in small populations. Evolution (change in gene frequencies) by chance processes alone.

Genetic equilibrium The maintenance of allele frequencies at the same genic selection, occurring by the differential propagation of different alleles with a population. A form of natural selection in which the frequency of an allele is determined by its rate of propagation relative to that of other alleles, averaged over the variety of genotypes in that population. See individual selection, kin selection, natural selection.

Genetic fitness The contribution by one genotype to the next generation in a population, relative to the contributions of other genotypes. By definition, the process of natural selection leads eventually to the prevalence of genotypes with the highest fitness.

Genetic load The average loss of genetic fitness in a population due to the presence of individuals less fit than others.

Genetic polymorphism The stable coexistence of two or more discontinuous genotypes in a population. When the frequencies of two alleles are maintained in equilibrium, the condition is called balanced polymorphism.

Genome The array of genes or the complete genetic constitution carried by an individual.

Genotype The set of genes possessed by an individual organism or the specific allelic or genetic composition of an organism with reference either to a single trait or to a set of traits under investigation (contrast with phenotype).

Genus (plural genera) A group of related, similar species (e.g., *Homo* the only extant species being *H. sapiens sapiens*).

Geographic race See subspecies.

Grade A level of phenotypic organization achieved by one or more species during evolution.

Group In biological terms, any set of organisms, belonging to the same species, that remain together for a period of time while interacting with one another to a distinctly greater degree than with other nonspecific organisms. A taxonomic "group" is also frequently used in a loose sense to refer to a set of related species (e.g., a genus or a division of a genus).

Group selection Selection that operates on two or more members of a linage group as a unit including both kin selection and interdemic selection. Broadly, the differential rate of origination or extinction of whole populations (or species) on the basis of differences among them in one or more characteristics. See heterozygous advantage.

Habitat The physical environment and the organisms contained in a particular place.

Half-life The amount of time required for one-half of the atoms in a radioactive element to decay. The measure of half-life is utilized in several fossil dating techniques.

Haploid A cell or organism having a single set of unpaired chromosomes and is also the gametic chromosome number.

Hardy-Weinberg law The principle that both gene and genotypic frequencies will remain in equilibrium in an indefinitely large population in the absence of mutation, migration, selection, and nonrandom mating. The Hardy-Weinberg law is used in studies of microevolution as a test for the null-hypothesis that change is not occurring in a population.

Heritability The fraction of variation of a trait within a population. Heritability is statistically measured by the fraction of its variance which is due to heredity as opposed to environmental influences. A heritability score of zero means that all the variation is due to the environment.

Heterosis The superiority of a heterozygote over either homozygote for a given trait.

Heterozygote An individual organism that possesses different alleles at one or more loci. Such individuals will produce unlike gametes and will not breed true.

Heterozygous advantage The manifestation of higher fitness by heterozygotes at a specific locus than by homozygotes at the same locus.

HLA Cell surface proteins which are involved in the acceptance or rejection of tissue and organ grafts and transplants. The proteins are produced by histocompatibility loci.

Homeostasis The maintenance of a steady state (a physiological or social steady state) via self-regulation through internal feedback responses.

Hominid A member of the family Hominidae (e.g., australopithecines and humans).

Hominoid A member of the superfamily Hominoidea (apes and humans).

Homo The genus of true humans, characterized by completely erect stature, bipedal locomotion, reduced dentition, and above all by an enlarged brain. The genus *Homo* includes several extinct forms (*H. habilis, H. erectus, H. neanderthalensis*), as well as modern humans (*H. sapiens sapiens*).

Homologous A similarity of form and structure between two species that they share with their nearest common ancestor.

Homozygote An individual which has identical alleles at one or more loci (at each of its gene copies). Such individuals will produce identical gametes and will consequently breed true.

Hybrid The product of crossing two parents of different genotypes.

Immunoglobin The class of serum proteins which have the properties of antibodies.

Inbreeding Mating between closely related organisms (kin). The degree of inbreeding is measured by the fraction of genes that are identical owing to common descent. (See inbreeding coefficient; and contrast with outcrossing.)

Inbreeding coefficient The probability that both alleles (gene forms) on one locus on a pair of chromosomes are identical by common descent, symbolized by f or F.

Inbreeding depression A loss or reduction in fitness, usually accompanying inbreeding of organisms.

Inclusive fitness The sum of an individual's own fitness plus all influence on fitness in its relatives other than direct descendants; the total effect of kin selection with reference to an individual.

Incomplete dominance The expression of a heterozygous phenotype in the offspring which is distinct from, and often intermediate to, that of either parent.

Independent assortment The independent segregation of each pair of homologous chromosomes during meiosis I. The random distribution of genes on different chromosomes into gametes.

Interdemic selection Group selection of populations with a species.

Isolating mechanism Any barrier to the exchange of genes between different populations of a group of organisms. Isolation can be classified as spatial, environmental, or reproductive.

K selection Selection favoring superiority in stable, predictable environments in which rapid population growth is unimportant. K selected species often have smaller numbers of offspring at a given time and usually provide more infant care than do r selected species (contrast with r selection).

Kin selection A form of genic selection in which alleles differ in their rate of propagation by influencing the survival or reproduction of individuals who carry the same alleles via a common ancestor.

Kinship The possession of a common ancestor in the relatively recent past. Kinship is measured precisely by the coefficient of kinship and coefficient of relationship.

Lineage group In general, a group of species allied by a common descent. Among humans, a group of individuals allied by common descent.

Linkage Occurrence of two loci on the same chromosome. They are functionally linked only if they are so close together on the chromosome that they do not segregate independently in meiosis.

Linkage equilibrium and **linkage disequilibrium** The state where two alleles at two or more loci are associated more or less frequently than predicted by their individual frequencies (contrast with linkage equilibrium).

Locus Specifically, a site on the chromosome occupied by a specific gene. Also loosely referred to as the gene itself, in all its allelic states.

Macroevolution A vague term for the evolution of great phenotypic changes usually resulting in the classification of the changed lineage and its descendants as another distinct genus or higher taxon.

Map unit In genetics, the measure of the distance between two genes, corresponding to a recombination frequency of 1%.

Maternal effect Phenotypic effects on the offspring produced by the maternal genome transmitted through the egg cytoplasm.

Maternal inheritance The transmission of traits via cytoplasmic genetic factors present in the egg cell but not in the sperm (e.g., mitochondria or chloroplasts).

MHC-Major Histocompatibility Complex Genetically determined tissue antigens; in humans, the HLA complex; and in mice, the H2 complex.

Microevolution A term for slight evolutionary changes within species, consisting of minor alterations in gene populations, chromosome structure, or chromosome numbers. (Note: A large amount of change would be referred to as macroevolution or simply as evolution.)

Mitochondrion A cytoplasmic organelle found in the cells of eukaryotes. These organelles are self-reproducing and the site of ATP synthesis.

Molecular clock A technique for determining dates of evolutionary divergences using bimolecular similarities and differences in extant species. The basic assumption of the technique is that molecular evolution proceeds at a fairly constant rate.

Monomorphic A population in which almost all the individuals have the same genotype at a locus (contrast with polymorphism).

Monophyletic group A group containing all known descendants of an ancestral species; usually the common ancestor that would be classified as a member of the group.

Morphocline The arrangement of the morphological variations of a homologous character into a continuum. The continuum of morphological variations is from the primitive to derived states.

Multiregional evolution hypothesis A highly controversial hypothesis of the evolution of modern human traits from multiple geographical regions, in contrast to a single African origin. Leading proponents are M. H. Wolpoff and A. T. Thorpe, among others. Also known as the candelabra hypothesis.

Mutation The process which produces an alteration in DNA or chromosome structure. Mutation is one of the causal agents of genetic variation.

Natural selection The differential survival and/or reproduction of classes of entities (alleles, genotypes or subsets of genotypes) such that the difference in survival and/or reproduction exceeds that expected by chance alone and results in an alteration of the proportions of different entities. Natural selection may also be viewed as the differential contribution of offspring to the next generation by individuals of different genetic types but belonging to the same population. This is the basic mechanism proposed by Charles Darwin, the mechanism or main guiding force in evolution and speciation. (See also genetic selection, individual selection, kin selection, group selection.)

Nearest-neighbor analysis A molecular technique utilized to determine the frequency with which nucleotides are adjacent to each other in polynucleotide chains.

Negative feedback A dynamic relation in which the product of a process inhibits the process that produces it. In biochemical processes, negative feedback usually enhances stability.

Norm of reaction In genetics, the set of phenotypic expressions of a genotype under different environmental conditions.

Normal distribution A probability function that approximates the distribution of random variables. The normal distribution is displayed graphically by the normal curve, also known as a Gaussian or bell-shaped curve.

Orthognathous In reference to the skull, having a relatively vertical and nonprotruding face (contrast with prognathous).

Perzygotic isolation mechanism All factors that reduce inbreeding by preventing courtship, mating, or fertilization.

Phenotype The observable properties of an organism (including morphological, physiological, biochemical, behavioral, and other properties of an organism), as they have developed under the combined influences of the genetic constitution of the individual and the effects of environmental factors (contrast with genotype).

Phyletic gradualism The model of evolution whereby change takes place slowly and in small steps; for contrast see punctuated equilibrium.

Phylogenetic tree See phylogram.

Phylogeny The evolutionary history or genealogical relationships among a group of organisms.

Phylogram A branching diagram for a set of species depicting their ancestral relationships. The vertical axis in such diagrams represents time (also called a **phylogenetic tree**).

Pleiotropism The control of more than one phenotypic characteristic (e.g., eye color, courtship behavior, or size) by the same gene or set of genes.

Point mutation A mutation resulting from a small, localized alteration in the chemical structure of a gene and can be mapped to a single locus; more specifically at the molecular level, a mutation that results in the substitution of one nucleotide for another.

Polymorphism Polymorphism is the maintenance of two or more forms of a gene (the rarest of which exceeds some arbitrarily low frequency—say 1%) on the same locus at higher frequencies than would be expected by mutation and immigration alone. The term may also more rarely be used to describe the existence within a population of phenotypic variation within a population, whether or not genetically based.

Pongid A member of the family Pongidae, the great apes (chimpanzees, gorillas, and orangutans).

Population A group of conspecific organisms (a group of interacting and actually or potentially interbreeding organisms that exhibits reproductive continuity from generation to generation) and occupies a delimited space at the same time. A group of populations of the same species, each occupying a different area, is sometimes called a metapopulation.

Postcranial skeleton All of the lower skeleton below the skull, that is, the limbs and vertebral column.

Postorbital bar The bony ring surrounding the lateral side of the orbit found in lower primates and many other mammals.

Potassium-argon (K/A) dating A radiometric technique for dating rocks which utilizes the amount of decay of potassium to argon.

Preadaptation Any pre-existing anatomical structure, physiological process, or behavioral pattern that makes new forms of evolutionary adaptation more likely (contrast with adaptation and postadaptation).

Primitive In evolutionary terms, primitive refers to a trait that appeared first in evolution and gave rise to other, more "advanced" traits later. Often primitive traits are less complex than later (or advanced) traits, but not always.

Probability The ratio of the frequency of a specific event to the frequency of all possible events.

Punctuated equilibrium A recent evolutionary model in which changes leading to new species may occur quickly. In this model, abrupt genetic shifts occur rather than slow and gradual change; for contrast, see also phyletic gradualism.

Quantum speciation The formation of a new species in a very short period of time (within a single or a few generations) by a combination of selection or drift.

R selection Selection favoring rapid rates of population increase. This type of selection is particularly prominent in species that specialize in colonizing short-lived environments or in species which undergo large fluctuations in population size (contrast with k selection).

Race A poorly defined term for a set of populations occupying a particular region that differs in one or more characteristics from populations elsewhere. A biological race is equal to **subspecies**. In some writings, a distinctive phenotype, whether or not allopatric from others.

Radiometric dating A group of techniques that make use of the fact that many kinds of atoms are unstable and change spontaneously into a lower energy state by radioactive emission. Each radioactive element has one particular mode of decay and its own unique rate of decay, which is constant. These techniques measure the ratios of undecayed atoms of the products of decay and extrapolate back to obtain the ages of many fossil-bearing rocks.

Random mating Mating of individuals without apparent regard to genotype.

Recombination The repeated formulation of new combinations of genes through the processes of meiosis and fertilization which occurs in organisms which reproduce sexually.

Restriction endonuclease Nuclease enzyme that recognizes specific nucleotide sequences in a DNA molecule, and cleaves the DNA at that site. Derived from a variety of microorganisms, those enzymes cleave both strands of the DNA and are used in the construction of recombinant DNA molecules.

Sagittal crest The bony crest running along the midline of the skull of certain primates and extinct Hominids (e.g., *Gorilla gorilla* and *Australopithecus bosei*) for the attachment of enlarged temporlis muscles.

Savanna The biome characterized by a flat plain of coarse grasses and scattered tree growth and in which rainfall is seasonal.

Selection The force responsible for changes in the frequency of alleles and genotypes in populations through differential reproduction.

Selection coefficient (s) A quantitative measure of the relative fitness of one genotype as compared with others.

Sexual dimorphism The phenomenon in which physical, homologous, and nonreproductive structures are of greatly different size and/or shape in males and females of the same species.

Sexual selection The differential ability of individuals of different genetic types to acquire mates. There are two basic types of sexual selection: (1) epigamic selection, based on choices made between males and females, and (2) intrasexual selection, based on competition between members of the same sex.

Speciation The processes of the genetic diversification of populations and the multiplication or creation of new species.

Species In the strict biological sense, the members in aggregate of a group of populations that interbreed or potentially interbreed with each other under natural conditions and that are reproductively isolated from other such groups. The basic lower category of classification in biological taxonomy, consisting of a population or series of populations of closely related and similar organisms which often but not always corresponds to the biological species.

Stabilization selection Selection which tends to stabilize the population around the mean by operating against the extremes of variation in a population (contrast with directional selection and disruptive selection).

Subspecies A subdivision of a species, usually defined narrowly as a geographical race that share one or more distinctive features. A population or series of populations occupying a discrete range and differing genetically from other geographical races of the same species.

Systematics Within a taxonomy, the study of the genetic and historical evolutionary relationships among organisms including their phenotypic similarities and differences.

Taxon (pl. taxa) The taxonomic unit (e.g., *Homo sapiens sapiens,* Hominidae, or Mammalia) to which individuals, groups of organisms, or sets of species, are classified.

Taxonomic rank The position of a taxon in the Linnaean hierarchy of classification: phylum, class, order, family, etc.

Thermoluminescence dating A technique for dating the age of quartz containing rocks and fossils embedded in that rock. The technique measures the number of alpha particles produced by radiation trapped in crystal lattices between the present and the last heating of the quartz crystal.

Transposable element A defined length of DNA that translocates to other sites in the genome, independent of sequence homology. Such elements are usually neighbors to short, inverted repeats of 20 to 40 base pairs at each end. The significance of translocation is the creation of new DNA sequences (e.g., insertion into a structural gene can produce a mutant phenotype). Insertion and excision is accomplished via two enzymes, transposase and resolvase. Transposable elements have been found in both prokaryotes and eukaryotes.

Type locality The site from which the type specimen for a type species or rock unit was taken.

Type species   The species for which a taxon (genus or higher-level) was initially named and described.

Uranium-lead dating   The radiometric dating technique used to date fossils that measures the decay of uranium into lead.

Variable region   Portions of immunoglobulin molecule that contain many amino acid sequence differences occurring between antibodies of differing specificities.

Viability   The number of individuals in a given phenotypic class that survive, measured in relation to another class (usually the wild type).

Wild type   The most prevalent allele, genotype, or phenotype in wild populations; with reference to the wild type allele; other alleles are often termed mutations.

Y chromosome   The male sex chromosome in species where the male is heterogametic (XY).

Zygomatic arch   The arch formed by projections of the zygomatic bone and the temporal bone on the lateral part of the skull for attachment of the masseter muscle.

Basic Statistical Terminology

MEAN: The mean is calculated by summing all observations and dividing by the total number of observations. A general formula for the mean is:

$$\bar{x} = \Sigma X_i / n$$

where
"x bar" is the mean
ΣX_i is the sum of all observations
n is the number of observations

STANDARD DEVIATION: The standard deviation is one measure of variation in the sample. If a sample is distributed normally, approximately two-thirds of the observations will fall within one standard deviation of EITHER side of the mean. For example, if the mean is 55.0 and the standard deviation is 10.0 then about two-thirds of the sample is between 45 and 65. In addition, 95% of all observations should fall within two standard deviations on each side of the mean, and 99% within 3 standard deviations of the mean. The general formula for the standard deviation is:

$$s = \sqrt{\sum (X_i - \bar{x})^2 / (n-1)}$$

SIGNIFICANCE LEVEL: The cutoff level for rejection or acceptance of a hypothesis. This is expressed as a percentage that represents the probability that you will reject a null hypothesis when it is TRUE. For example, with a significance level of 5% you will reject a true null in 1 out of 20 experiments. At a significance level of 1% you will reject a true null in 1 out of 100 experiments. When the significance level is expressed as a frequency, it is called the α- or p-level (where 5% = 0.05 and 1% = 0.01).

CATEGORICAL VARIABLES: Qualitative data that fall into two or more mutually exclusive categories (y or n, male vs. female, red, white, or yellow). To treat such variables statistically, they are expressed as frequencies.

DISCRETE VARIABLES: Quantitative observations that are not on a continuous scale (for example, the number of young born in a litter). Numerically discrete variables assume a limited number of values with no intermediate values possible (a litter will not contain 1.23 young).

CONTINUOUS VARIABLES: Quantitative observations that are measured over a continuous range. These include measurements such as length, area, and volume that can theoretically assume an infinite number of values.

T-TEST: A test used to determine if there is a statistically significant difference between the mean of two samples that are measured quantitatively.

CHI-SQUARE TEST: A test used to determine if there is a statistically significant difference among the frequencies of categorical variables.

DEGREES OF FREEDOM: Used in statistical testing to account for the increased likelihood of biased sampling when sample sizes are small. Degrees of freedom are calculated as n–1, where n is the sample size.

Using Microsoft Excel for Statistical Calculations

1. Enter your data from each group you are analyzing into separate columns of the Microsoft Excel worksheet.

2. To perform an arithmetic or statistical function, go to an empty cell on the worksheet and type an = sign. This will activate the formula bar, which is located at the top of the screen.

3. Hit the *fx* (function wizard) button which will display the function names. Click on the correct function, for example STDEV to calculate the standard deviation. You will then be prompted to give the location within the worksheet for the sample of interest. Click on the worksheet to highlight the cells containing your sample. (NOTE: You may see several lines to enter your samples on. You only need to fill out the line for number 1 on your sample.)

4. Press enter and the calculation will appear in the cell.

Additional Data for t-Tests

1. Each of your samples is entered separately into the box as array 1 and array 2.

2. The number of tails to use will be 2.

3. Under type of t-test enter a 2.

4. The number calculated is the p-value of the test. If the significance was set at 0.05 and this number is GREATER then you must accept the null hypothesis. If the calculated p-value is = or less than 0.05 then you can reject the null hypothesis and accept the alternative.

Chi-Square Analysis

If we hypothesize that a trait is inherited in a particular way, we will expect to see a certain phenotypic ratio in the offspring of a specific cross. Chi-squares determine if deviations from the expected ratios are great enough to reject the hypothesis. The following examples will show you how to perform a chi-square analysis.

Let's say we were looking at eye color in humans and we hypothesized that this trait was inherited in a simple dominant-recessive manner with brown eyes dominant to blue eyes. If we looked at many monohybrid crosses (both parents heterozygous), we would expect a phenotypic ratio of 3:1 in the offspring. When we test this hypothesis, we look at 100 offspring and find that 68 have brown eyes and 32 have blue eyes. This is close to, but not exactly a 3:1 ratio. Is this deviation significant? First we fill out a table with the number we EXPECTED from our hypothesis vs. the number actually OBSERVED.

Eye color

Phenotypes	# Observed	# Expected	Chi-square
Brown	68	75	
Blue	32	25	
Total	100	100	

Now we calculate the chi-square values for each trait with the formula:

$$\text{(observed-expected)}^2/\text{expected} = \text{chi-square}$$

In this case, we get 0.65 for brown and 1.96 for blue eyes. For the total chi-square value, we add together our calculated chi-square values and get 2.61.

Eye color

Phenotypes	# Observed	# Expected	Chi-square
Brown	68	75	0.65
Blue	32	25	1.96
Total	100	100	2.61

If we are only looking at the ratios of two alleles, than the deviation is insignificant and the hypothesis is supported if the total chi-square value is <2.7. Total chi-square values >2.7 mean the deviation is significant and we should reject the hypothesis. Will you reject or accept the hypothesis?

Note: The cutoff for rejection or acceptance can vary depending on how stringently you test your hypothesis. Our hypothesis (null hypothesis) is that there is no difference between the observed and expected values. Here we are using a stringency of $p = 0.10$. This represents a probability level where 10% of the time we will reject the null hypothesis when it is true.